The Artist's State of Mind

of Mind

A Guide to Accessing the Flow State Through Mastery of Your Chosen Craft

Jax Pax

"Australian-born author and songwriter Jax Pax has thought deeply about what happens when we stretch ourselves to the limits of our ability and how it pays off in both quality of performance and enjoyment of what we're doing. He shares more practical wisdom than many much longer books.

Whether you're an artist or a craftsperson, or you want to approach whatever you do with that kind of attention and care, read *The Artist's State of Mind: A Guide to Accessing the Flow State Through Mastery of Your Chosen Craft* slowly and reflectively. Its relaxed prose will speak to you with insights and strategies you can apply immediately to achieve mastery of your work and yourself."

Gary Gute
Creativity and Flow Researcher
TheFlowChannel.com

"The Artist's State of Mind by Jax Pax delivers on its title and more. It's short enough to read in one sitting, but I took a few weeks with it because I admired it as a sound introduction to how artists prepare for their best work, then carry through. Concise. Thoughtful. The author has consolidated lessons from longer works to simplify them for anyone desiring mastery, but this book is particularly friendly to beginners. Pax's observations and insights as a songwriter showcase songwriting as a metaphor for all sorts of creative skills.

Read the table of contents and you'll know if it's for you. I liked it. It reminded me how much attitude affects the work, and that artists can choose a state of mind that calls up creativity."

Marshall Vandruff
Art Teacher and Illustrator
MarshallArt.com and the Proko Channel on YouTube

Table of Contents

Introduction

Have you ever wondered why some people love a particular activity so much while others despise it? Why is one man's lifestyle trash, another man's treasure? Aside from the influence of cultural experiences and character, the answer lies in understanding the nature of enjoyment and the flow state, which will be the overarching theme of this book. There are some things in life that are automatically enjoyable, while others are an acquired taste. As will be discussed in detail, the immensely enjoyable state we call *flow* is something that most often comes when advanced skills are met with an appropriate challenge. One that is high, but not too high.

Throughout this book I have mentioned many crafts from music to sports to the path of scientific discovery, but I have focused mainly on the art of songwriting as that is the art form I've had most experience with having been an acoustic guitar enthusiast (though not a virtuoso by any means) for around 16 years and having been writing for around a decade. However, the concepts throughout this book can be applied to *any* craft. Additionally, what is learnt through the chosen craft can be applied by analogy to other areas of the reader's life. If I've succeeded in my intentions, what took me years to learn through experience, through trial and error, and through researching Eastern philosophy and high-performance psychology, will be conveyed to the reader within a matter of hours throughout this short book.

Not every craft is commonly thought of as an art form. Some crafts are even purely internal such as critical thinking which can be approached in the way described throughout this book also. So, I want to point out that I am using the term 'artistry' very loosely and you don't need to be an art lover in any way to benefit from reading

8

The Artist's State of Mind. The same principles can be applied to the pursuit of mastery in sports or science also.

The Artist's State of Mind has been written as a series of small essays so that it can either be read cover to cover or simply dipped into for a ten-minute read now and then as each section is pretty much a standalone. For maximum benefit though, I recommend reading it through cover to cover, then reading through a second time after the concepts have been swimming around in your mind for a few months. I, as the author, still benefit from reviewing sections of this book as the concepts sink a little further into my way of life and my way of seeing things each time I remind myself of those concepts. I have done my best to distil the practical side of Eastern philosophy and of high performance psychology so that you can investigate these concepts without having to waste time rummaging through piles of dogma and folklore.

The Artist's State of Mind begins with an introduction to the flow state; what it is and how it can be achieved. This is followed by a discussion of performance psychology and human potential and an argument is made against the myth of *innate* genius. Next, some thoughts on how to approach practice most effectively and how to reach integrity in your chosen field. From there, it's onto a closer look at the flow state and the building blocks of the optimal mindset required for high performance and enjoyment. An in-depth deconstruction of the creative process is then laid out before a closer look at the key roadblocks that stand in the way of high performance and mastery. *The Artist's State of Mind* finishes with a discussion of non-dual perception, the ultimate condition of the flow state that

brings all of the above together.

Flow

What is Flow?

"When the foot touches the ground, the foot feels the foot."

–Buddha

The flow state is spoken of in many different ways. Popularly referred to as the 'Zen state', or as being 'in the zone', we most often speak of this profound state when referring to experiences we've had during sports or other recreation when the time flew by and the mind and body were at one. In Zen, such an occurrence is said to be an observer-less state, as the person is unaware of being in the state while it's happening. Only afterwards, do they look back and realize that time had disappeared and the body-mind had acted as if of its own accord, effortlessly executing the task at hand—be it scoring a goal in sports, building a project, reading a book, getting lost in conversation, or any other activity.

What many people don't realize is that the sort of deep enjoyment they get from their favorite activity is not something that is unique to that particular activity, but rather it is a state of mind that has fallen upon them due to the way that the activity has been approached. Almost any activity can be approached in such a way. This 'way' is so elusive that it's often referred to in eastern philosophy as, "the way of no way". The tradition of Taoism is built around this observer-less state of mind that cannot be reached reliably through any particular method.

However, Mihaly Csikszentmihalyi, the renowned psychologist and author of *Flow,* has found that there are particular conditions that make *flow* more likely to occur. Csikszentmihalyi writes:

> We have seen how people describe the common characteristics of optimal experience; a sense that one's skills are adequate to cope with the challenges at hand, in a goal-directed action system that provides clear clues as to how well one is performing [...] Flow occurs when skills and challenges are both high and are equaling each other.[1]

As Mihaly suggests, the level of challenge must be high but not *too* high. The sweet spot is just at the edge of the person's ability. It is in that situation that attention is focused and the duality of the observer and the observed is sublimated as there is no space left to think about oneself. It's like a disappearing act in which the sense of self is gone from view and only the task at hand remains. World class snowboarder, Shaun White, describes his experience of the flow state while performing near impossible maneuvers such as the tomahawk: "At that point you're really not thinking, you're just letting it happen. It's a mixture of being completely focused, then slightly not caring."

There is an interesting and unexpected benefit that comes with having experienced the flow state. When the person returns to ordinary self-consciousness they often find that they have let themselves go a little more. The result is an unexpected leap in personal growth. This fascinating interplay between flow and ego is key to development both as a person and as an artist. Those who are aware of this interplay between ego and flow often express their gratitude for those moments when flow has found them and their work has benefited in ways that could never have been thought up consciously. In Tim Ferriss's book, *Tools of Titans*, the famous filmmaker, Robert Rodriguez, talks about his experience with flow:

> You get in your own way — thinking that you needed to know something, a trick or a process, before it would flow. If you got out of the way, it would just flow. What gives you permission to let it flow? Sometimes if you take four years of schooling or you study under somebody, then you've suddenly given yourself permission to let it flow....
>
> You're just opening up the pipe and creativity flows through. And as soon as your ego

gets in the way, and you go, 'I don't know if I know what to do next', you've already put 'I' in front of it and you've already blocked it a little bit. 'I did it once, but I don't know if I can do it again.' It was never you. The best you can do is just to get out of the way so it comes through.

When an actor comes to me and says, 'I'm not sure I know how to play this part,' I say, 'That's beautiful because the other half's gonna show up when we're there.' They say knowing is half the battle. I think the most important part is the other part — not knowing what's going to happen but trusting that it will be there when you put the brush up to the canvas. It's going to know where to go… The trust comes first.[2]

Being in the zone is not just the optimal way to achieve high performance; it's an end in itself. The flow state is characteristically accompanied by blissful enjoyment. Surgeons have described the flow state as being accompanied by "a sense that the entire operating team is a single organism, moved by the same purpose and all involved share in a feeling of harmony and power."[3] This particular description of flow during surgery is similar to that reported by musicians playing in bands. Not only do musicians report feeling as if they are one while playing together, but they also report experiencing a sort of floating sensation as if the body were buoyant.

Mastery and Flow

"I would have made a great deal of money in corporate life, but I realized one day that I wasn't enjoying it. I wasn't having the kinds of experiences that make life rewarding. I saw that my priorities were mixed up, spending most of my hours in the office [...] The years were slipping by. I enjoy being a carpenter. I live where it's quiet and beautiful and I climb almost every night. I figure that my own relaxation and availability will mean more to my family than the material things I can no longer give them."[4]

−A former businessman who moved to the mountains to pursue carpentry

Throughout the ages, craftspeople and innovators have gained insight into the workings of the mind — and how enjoyment comes about — by exploring their craft and by observing the *flow* state as it occurs in the execution of the master's craft. By studying the *process* itself, we will uncover ways of making the flow state a more common occurrence than it would otherwise be.

Without developing a high level of skill in an art form, sport, or other activity, flow would be a very rare occurrence. As the artist refines her craft, the mind is being refined also. Remaining present during very finely focused practice seems to demand an enormous amount of energy, but the benefits are enormous too. After a day of intense, focused practice a craftsperson will often find their mind is sharpened. Even something as simple as taking a walk in the park becomes a beautiful experience. The light and the life in the park seem to be felt rather than just perceived. Josh Waitzkin, who has been world champion in both tai chi push hands (a form of martial art) and in chess puts it beautifully in his book, *The Art of Learning*:

[The advantages to such condensing practice extend far beyond the professional and competitive arenas. If you are driving your car, crossing the street, or doing any other mundane activity, and are suddenly confronted by a potentially dangerous situation, if you are trained to perform optimally on a moment's notice, then you may emerge unscathed from some hair-raising situations. But far more important than these rare climactic explosions, I believe that this type of condensing practice can do wonders to raise our quality of life. Once a simple inhalation can trigger a state of tremendous alertness, our moment-to-moment awareness becomes blissful, like that of someone half-blind who puts on glasses for the first time. We see more as we walk down the street. The everyday becomes exquisitely beautiful. The notion of boredom becomes alien and absurd as we naturally soak in the lovely subtleties of the "banal." All experiences become richly intertwined by our new vision, and then new connections begin to emerge. Rainwater streaming on a city pavement will teach a pianist how to flow. A leaf gliding easily with the wind will teach a controller how to let go. A house cat will teach me how to move. All moments become each moment […] Presence has taught me how to live.[5]

Through the pursuit of mastery, the apprentice does not only learn the skill that is directly being practiced, but also learns the workings of the mind in general. He or she is learning how to learn. This can potentially lead to a more skillful use of the mind in all activities, and can deepen the person's ability to face life's challenges. As you get to know your craft, you get to know the mind.

A further benefit of mastery is that, when the mastery process is approached with care, the resulting increase in understanding of the mind can lead to a greater sense of self-reliance and a reduction in psychological dependency. Most people are reliant on the distractions created by chemical entertainment or by being constantly busy to keep their life focused. Leisure time is perceived by many people as boring and as a time to self-medicate, to drown out the storm of thoughts.

Such people unconsciously cling to toxic relationships as they prefer anything over the turmoil of facing the flood of their own thoughts that comes when they are alone. However, a better understanding of, and relationship with, the mind leads to a life where boredom is replaced by intrigue and serenity. Boredom is rarely encountered by a person whose mind has been well-developed, provided that they are healthy and spending the majority of their time with the freedom to use their mind as they please.

As the beginner learns to overcome challenges in mastering a skill, he or she realizes that often situations that initially seem impossible to overcome can in fact be worked through with the right approach. In this way, the pursuit of mastery provides a vehicle for personal growth.

Genius is Not Innate

"Our infirmities help us unexpectedly."

–William James

"It's not that I'm so smart; it is just that I stay with

problems longer."

–Albert Einstein

In life, most of us feel as if we are part of a world in which there is a sort of hierarchy of intelligence with the average person being well below that of the geniuses who have invented our machinery and computers, who've made the greatest discoveries, and who've created the most beautiful (or maybe only popular) art works. We are led to believe that those geniuses have been endowed with genetic qualities that have granted them some sort of innate brain function that processes and computes at a level beyond what a normal mind is capable of. But did they pull off those achievements due to an innate mental processing ability similar to that of a computer, or do we need to fine-tune our definition of what genius is?

Renowned psychologist Anders Ericsson has spent his career studying high-performance athletes, prodigies, and high achievers in many fields and has come to the conclusion that:

> [...] among those people who have practiced enough and have reached a certain level of skill in their chosen field, there is no evidence that any genetically determined abilities play a role in deciding who will become the best. Once you get

to the top, it isn't natural talent that makes the difference, at least not "talent" in the way it is usually understood as an innate ability to excel at a particular activity.[6]

Ericsson is not alone in his claim that innate talent is a sham. For example, the Hungarian psychologist László Polgár had studied the progression of hundreds of people who were considered to be geniuses in their fields and concluded that with the right nurture almost anyone *of normal intelligence* could be trained to reach genius level in a chosen field.[7] In the late 1960's, he and his wife Klara set out to prove this by raising their three daughters to become chess prodigies.

At the time, many chess fanatics believed a woman could never excel at chess. This made the experiment all the more impactive when all three of the girls did in fact go on to have enormous success in chess. At fifteen, their first daughter became the highest ranked female chess player in the world, and she then went on to become the first woman to be awarded with grandmaster status via the same path as males take. Their second daughter was given one of the highest single-tournament ratings ever for either a male or a female chess player. The occasion is known amongst chess players as "The Sack of Rome" and is still talked about in the chess world today — more than two decades later.

If this wasn't enough to prove the parents' point, the success of the Polgár's third daughter, Judit, surely would. Judit was awarded with grandmaster status at just fifteen years and five months, making her at the time, the youngest person, male or female, to ever be awarded as grandmaster.[8] She was then the highest ranked female chess player in the world for the next twenty-five years before deciding to retire from chess. There was a time when she was ranked number eight in the world among all chess players, male or female. In 2005, she was the first and only woman in history to compete in the overall World Chess Championships. And so, the Polgárs had shown, with very strong evidence, that mastery is more a result of effective nurture than of supernormal nature. The legacy of the Polgárs is further supported by scientific studies that show adult chess players have no better visuospatial abilities than normal non-chess playing adults, neither do they have higher IQ's than other adults with similar levels of education.[9] [10]

Another legend that comes up in relation to super-normal intelligence is Savant Syndrome. We've all heard stories of people with savant-like abilities: a person who has memorized the entire phone book, someone who can perform incredible math calculations as quickly as a computer, a musical prodigy, and so on. But what is often missing from these stories of seemingly superhuman skill is that behind the skill lies many hours of intensely focused practice coupled with an uncommon obsession with a very narrow interest that most people would never be willing to give much time to. Researchers, Francesca Happé and Pedro Vital, have studied autistic children who develop savant-like abilities and compared them with autistic children who do not develop such abilities. They have concluded that the abilities of autistic savants arise as the result of a combination of their attention to detail and their exclusive focus on the particular 'special interest' that possesses them. Or in other words: they've worked for their talents just like everyone else.[11]

Now that this notion of innate genius has been loosened up, let's tackle the big guns — Albert Einstein. Einstein's achievements are so incredible that his name has pretty much become a simile for the word "genius" itself. It's not surprising that he is seen to have had a sort of alien-like level of intelligence considering that he did discover a whole new area of physics that pretty much completely changed our view of the universe. But even Einstein himself said, "I have no special talent; I am only passionately curious." So, if the man himself seemed to reject the idea of a human being having some sort of brain function that a normal human isn't capable of, there's our first clue in this puzzle.

Rather than viewing genius as an innate computational ability, it may be more accurate to say that genius is more of an *action* that has been accomplished as the result of a very passionate character meeting with the right community and situational forces. When a curious, determined and anti-authoritarian character meets with a rare opportunity, sometimes, after many years of work, that can lead to a breakthrough in science or art and that breakthrough itself, I believe, is what we could define as "genius". Not everybody has it. But it is a very particular thing. Not simply some generic superior brain-processing power.

Biographers have noted that Einstein was raised in an unusual family, and his mother reported that he would ignore social life while sitting alone for days on end, immersed in the search for a solution and not giving up until he had found it.[12] From age ten, Einstein began receiving tutoring from a local medical student who introduced him to a series of books by Aaron Bernstein called *People's Books on Natural Science*. Right from the first volume, Bernstein dealt with the speed of light. The famous thought experiment regarding a bullet shooting through the window of a moving train, that had influenced Einstein's work, was included in these books and Einstein later reported that he had devoured Bernstein's books with "breathless attention." Einstein later stated that Bernstein's book had exerted great influence on his whole development.

Einstein's marks at school in Aarau, showed that he had performed poorly not just in French but also in chemistry. His father said, "With Albert I got used to finding mediocre grades along with very good ones."[13] Later, at the Zurich Polytechnic, as strange as it sounds, Einstein scored only 4 out of 6 in most of his math courses including those in geometry, which had been an intense interest of his. Einstein later reported having been ignorant of the subtler part of mathematics and surprisingly he was actually reliant on help from a math professor when he was later forming his geometric theory of gravity. What may also surprise, is that Einstein's friend and mathematician, Marcel Grossman, helped him with the math he needed to turn his special theory of relativity into a general theory.[14]

After graduating from university, Einstein took on a particularly rare opportunity that would blend well with his interest in the nature of light and time. He was employed as an assistant patent clerk in a role that involved analyzing patents for time-keeping devices. This gave the young legend the opportunity to think about the nature of time almost constantly, and he spent much of the day pondering the nature of time and of light with an intense curiosity that it is easy to assume very few human beings would ever have had. His array of interests in light, time and physics went together perfectly well and at age twenty-six — after ten years of racking his brain on questions that perhaps very few human beings before him had ever pondered — Einstein had his first major breakthrough.

An intriguing question is: How many people in history had the combination of opportunities, situational forces, and *character traits* that led to Einstein's breakthrough? Okay, an obvious objection to this attempt to debunk innate genius is to say that it is the curious character itself that is the genius, rather than a mysterious brain-processing power. That, I have no objection to. Most importantly, I want to point out that genius is not to do with rare genetics or processing power, but, rather, it fits the fine-tuned definition above: when a curious, determined and anti-authoritarian character meets with a rare opportunity leading to a breakthrough innovation.

Another historical figure who is often used as an example of innate genius is the famous composer, Mozart. What is not so often mentioned though, is that Mozart's father was widely regarded as the best music teacher in all of Europe. It is quite likely that he benefited greatly from posting Mozart as a child prodigy as that would be beneficial to his own teaching business. If Mozart were not the greatest musician in Europe, then how could his father possibly maintain a reputation as the greatest teacher? Also of relevance is that although Mozart began composing at a very young age, he did not begin composing works of world-class expertise until later on when his skill had had time to develop.

What about Leonardo da Vinci then? Da Vinci is often talked about as being the most widely talented genius of all time, but he cops a lot of criticism too. When worshipped by his fans, Da Vinci is often credited as being an inventor, a painter, an engineer and so on. But critics are quick to mention that some of his inventions actually never would have worked. To bring it down to earth some more, it is worth pointing out that in modern times, a person is not thought to be an inventor until they have gone through the expensive process of securing a patent, while in contrast, Da Vinci merely had to sketch out his ideas and that automatically counted as inventing.

A further criticism of Da Vinci is that he had laborers working on his paintings with him. This is very common amongst famous artists. Andy Warhol, for example, didn't make all of his artworks himself. It is reasonable to assume that many so-called "ordinary" people would be capable of producing an impressive body of work if they had such a community supporting them. In Da Vinci's case, the enthusiasts respond by saying, "Da Vinci not only conceived of the images but he also had a touch that was a thousand times better than that of the laborers." The renowned neuroscientist, V.S. Ramachandran, plays with this by showing his students 3 sketches of a horse; one by a seven-year-old autistic girl named Nadia, who can't converse with people and struggles with ordinary daily tasks; a second by Leonardo da Vinci; and a third by a normal eight-year-old. He shows his students these 3 sketches without telling them who they were drawn by and surprisingly, more people prefer Nadia's beautifully drawn horse over Da Vinci's. (as a side note: ironically, when Nadia reached adolescence she matured and gained higher abilities, effectively becoming less autistic. She also lost her ability to draw. Ramachandran suggests that this may be evidence that formal education can stifle some creative abilities. This is also perhaps evidence that a human being has a limited amount of processing power, and that excelling in one area may mean stifling in another.)[15]

Rock music has a very powerful influence over our culture and hence rock stars are often posted as super-human geniuses also. It is often the musicians of the late 1900's and particularly of the '60's and '70's that get most of the applaud. Some say, nobody has created such a revolutionary sound as the early pioneers of rock music did. The story is commonly told as if they simply plucked their fresh sounds out of thin air. But this is a misperception that arises from various factors. Firstly, we don't hear much of the music that the '60's rock musicians were influenced by because there was a rapid increase in recording and broadcasting technologies happening around that time as well as the introduction of television into homes. Because the recordings of the '50's were lower in quality, we don't often hear that music these days and therefore, many people think that the music of the '60's was just created out of nowhere.

Secondly, there were a lot of technological advancements that enabled instruments to be played in innovative ways. For example, the invention of guitar distortion and modulating effects for guitars changed music in the '60's. Jimi Hendrix is often credited for being the first to use certain tones but this could be attributed to the fact that he had a friendship with Roger Mayer, an electronic engineer who invented for Hendrix use, the Axis fuzz unit, the Octavia Octave Doubler and a vibrato unit called the UniVibe. Yes, Hendrix was an astonishingly skilled and tasteful guitarist too, but this was not necessarily an innate processing ability. After all, he had spent about a decade touring as a roadie with the greatest blues guitarists of that era and learnt directly from them.

The third factor involved with the exaggeration of genius in regard to the explosion in music innovation in the '60's is that, due to various factors outside of the music industry, western culture was rapidly changing. Increasing globalization has led more and more to a loosening of social rules as people travel and become influenced by other cultures. So, by the late 60's, people no longer had to wear a suit on stage and be polite in their manner nor in their compositions or in their use of tones. Basically, music got ruder.

The Beatles made a large body of work and a fraction of it was outstanding. However, there are various unique opportunities to take into account that would negate the need to attribute *innate* genius to their success. I'm not saying the music itself wasn't genius. Nor am I suggesting that any random person could have produced it. But that genius quality of the music is not necessarily the result of an innate computing ability possessed by the individuals' brains. It can easily be explained as being the result of the emergent qualities of a specialized and focused community (the band etc.) in combination with passionate characters and the right situational forces.

The Beatles had gone to a high school that specialized in poetry. This gave them a head start in the lyric writing department. That was one factor that put them in a small league of their own to begin with. Another important factor to consider is that, back in those days, most people had relatively little access to music by comparison to what we have now. These days you could live almost anywhere in the industrialized world and still be able to access any music via the internet. But in the '60's when the Beatles were developing their skills as musicians many people around the world had fairly limited access to music. The Beatles first album was pretty unspectacular and not particularly innovative. In fact, it was recorded while John Lennon had a cold that affected his singing voice in a noticeable way. When this recording was well-received despite the unusual vocal tone created by John Lennon's sore throat, the Beatles realized something strange about recorded music: When people become familiar with something unusual, they begin to like it. This realization played a part in the band's approach to creativity from that time onward.

Once the Beatles had their initial success, many opportunities opened up that made it easier for them to access a wide range of music to be influenced by. For example, the Beatles once hired the virtuoso guitarist, John Fahey, and sat on the floor in front of him for days on end asking him to play parts of his music over and over again while they learnt how to imitate the techniques that Fahey had developed.

The Beatles also had the opportunity to travel in a time when traveling was not nearly as affordable for the average person as it is today. This led to them being influenced by Indian music and various other styles from around the world. Opportunities lead to more opportunities and it is not necessary to attribute a work of genius to *innate* ability. To do so would only insult the creator as it discredits their many years of diligent work. A work of genius is the result of an enormous amount of work, sometimes in combination with rare opportunities and, importantly also, a well-suited and passionate character and community.

It may seem a little over-confident to think I have completely debunked the possibility of innate supernormal brain function just with the reasoning above, but as mentioned earlier, there have been a number of esteemed psychologists who have studied high performers and have also come to the conclusion that genius is not innate. My goal is simply to loosen the grip that the notion of supernormal intelligence has on us. The belief in supernormal intelligence, I believe, leads to gullibility and a submissive way of life. If you have been feeling as if you are a part of some worldwide intellectual hierarchy, then why not open your mind to the possibility that with effective practice and education, you may have the potential to master the field you're interested in. To get to a world class level may be out of reach due to the necessity of having suitable opportunities, but as far as an individual's daily enjoyment goes, a world-class level of mastery or success isn't necessary. And that's what this book is about: Developing mastery, for the sake of enjoying daily life.

So, we have a lot of evidence to debunk the myth that "genius" arises from some sort of innate processing power. Some readers may still be thinking, "But all the people who've achieved deep mastery at their craft have possessed a very strong self-discipline that I don't have." Well, it is quite possible that having a drive for integrity or self-discipline may be genetic. This has not been proven nor disproven. But if you are deciding straight-up that you don't have that sort of drive, then you may be jumping the gun on this one. Many people are disciplined in one area and sloppy in other areas. Many world-class musicians, for example, had given up on various instruments before finding their preferred instrument and with it finding a source of unrealized energy and a respect for integrity. If you have not been deeply struck by anything yet then that doesn't mean that you never will. My favorite motto of all time is: *"Don't weigh your abilities by the success you've already had in life."*

If the masters had weighed their potential too early in life, they would never have been confident enough to pursue their dreams of mastery, and never would have developed the mastery they now wield. This is true for every person who has ever mastered anything.

For some people, the passion comes when they are in their youth; for others, it comes much later. It has been well and truly proven that the brain can develop right through into old age. You are never too old to begin on the way to mastery.

48

The Growth Mindset

The groundbreaking work of bestselling developmental psychologist, Carol Dweck, demonstrates that if there is one key difference between those who continue to thrive when faced by challenges and those who crumble: it's that those who thrive carry the "growth mindset" while those who crumble carry the "fixed mindset".[16]

A person carrying a growth mindset tends to perceive "talent" as something that has come through time and diligent practice, eventually leading to mastery. Conversely, someone with a fixed mindset, tends to see people as fixed entities. To a person with a fixed mindset, an individual is either "smart" or "stupid" or somewhere in between. Situational forces and the background education of the person being judged as either smart or stupid do not come to mind when talent is being weighed by a person carrying a fixed mindset.

In many cases, this belief in fixed qualities eventually backfires on a person who has grown up being labelled as "smart" unless they take the time to realize the advantages they've had and to understand what has led to their early life success. They may have been a big fish in a small pond, but unless they are happy to cease learning and growing, then they may need to learn to thrive as a little fish in a big pond. It's like the story of the tortoise and the hare. If a person becomes smug, they will eventually come up against a situation where their advantages will no longer pull them through unless they learn to work diligently toward growth.

Even the fixed-mindset itself, however, is not fixed. Depending on their belief system, a person can have a growth mindset in sports and a fixed mindset regarding "musical giftedness", for example. And, this too, can change over time.

Dweck has found that when challenged by difficult situations, people with the growth mindset are far more likely to pull-through than are those with a fixed mindset. She writes:

"The ones with the fixed mindset thought: 'If I have ability, I'll do well; If I don't, I won't.' As a result, they didn't use sophisticated strategies to help themselves. They just studied in an earnest but superficial way and hoped for the best."[17] Dweck also suggests that reassuring children about their intelligence or innate talent often backfires. When a child is praised in such a way, there is an underlying sense that their traits are being measured all the time, and so they are afraid of failure as failure would show a deficiency in their apparently fixed abilities.

So, in other words, when you compliment somebody's intelligence, you are unintentionally stunting their growth by encouraging a fixed mindset. To overcome this, and to instill a healthy work ethic in children, she recommends that teachers, coaches, and parents praise the *work* the children put in to achieve, rather than praising intelligence. Or in other words, praise the process rather than praising the achievement.

With a life focused on process rather than outcome, the child will grow to be more resilient, understanding and forward-moving. On the other hand, the mindset of living for achievements leads to a life-plan, in which the enjoyment of life is constantly being deferred until the end goal has been achieved. In a life focused purely on achievement daily life is a boring misery and the person is left with a constant feeling of being invalid and incomplete as they have not yet added the next achievement to their identity. As the esteemed gymnastics coach, Chris Sommers says, we'd be better off to *"Learn to enjoy and appreciate the process. You are going to spend far more time on the actual journey than with those all too brief moments of triumph at the end."*[18]

Another disadvantage that a person faces when carrying the fixed mindset is that it creates an attachment to their current identity and an urgent need to prove themself. Strange as it may seem, this attachment persists even if the trait the person is protecting is unwanted. George Mumford, author of *The Mindful Athlete* and former mindfulness coach to the Chicago Bulls, speaks of his experience with this attachment to victimhood that he has seen in the athletes he's worked with:

Sometimes we can become so attached to our suffering that we actually identify with it. Without our suffering, we don't know who we are, and so we unconsciously cling to it and ultimately create the thoughts, habits and actions that become our destiny [...]

I've worked with many people individually and in groups who have come to me for help, but who bail out when the going gets too tough. I understand why they leave: because they never get comfortable with being uncomfortable. In fact, many individuals want to change, but they're often unconsciously attached to their suffering, or to the old self they think they want to change. They have identified with the suffering or that old self for so long that they're afraid they won't know who they are without it — even if that suffering or that old self has no real place in the context of their current life anymore.[19]

There are benefits to be gained from victimhood, and therefore, many people become very attached to their problems. When life nudges them to change their ways and their perception of themselves, they mistakenly take that as an insult to "who they are".

Often the growth mindset of a person of advanced mastery has come about by way of necessity. When they first encountered their passion, the drive was so strong to attain mastery that there was no saying no. They simply had to get to work and stifling was never considered to be an option. But although individuals may differ in their basic character and in their temperaments and aspirations, we can all adapt the growth mindset to any area of life and of mastery. As the poet, Sekou Andrews, put it,

"You must want to be a butterfly so badly, you are willing to give up being a caterpillar."[20]

Practice

"The more present we are at practice, the more present we will be in competition, in the boardroom, at the exam, the operating table, the big stage."[21]

—*Josh Waitzkin*

Motivation

The attainment of mastery requires many hours of diligent practice and this at first can seem daunting. It's that awkward clumsiness and uncertainty that we experience when we take up something new that stands in the way of commitment to mastery. It's not much of a rub for the ego to witness ourselves being defeated by an activity as we clumsily make our attempts at it. Whether it's making a horrible sound on a musical instrument, losing a tournament, missing the archery target or dancing like a moron, the experience is never much better than mediocre. But without mastery, deep enjoyment will never come in most activities.

Maintaining the drive to push through those awkward stages that the beginner faces can be an art in itself. Fortunately, though, there are many ways to maintain motivation and to decrease the boredom, awkwardness and fears that are inevitably encountered on the road to mastery. Once the beginning stages are overcome, the pursuit becomes more enjoyable and there are periods of smooth progression. It becomes easier to practice as the foundational skills provide a ground for more advanced skills to be built upon and the craft becomes more enjoyable.

To maintain motivation, it's important to keep in mind the nature of the road to mastery itself. It is guaranteed that you will be clumsy and defeated in the beginning of the journey, and that you will then progress. You will come up against obstacles and plateaus and to your own astonishment, you will overcome those obstacles. Then the rewards of mastery will come — the enjoyment of the art form as an end in itself, and the enjoyment of the side benefits it offers too. A master chef not only enjoys the act of cooking but also enjoys a lucrative career, as well as a diet fit for a king. A master athlete enjoys playing her sport but also may enjoy a more prolific social life than she otherwise would have had. A fine wood craftsperson is able to use or to sell the furniture and other items she has built. But these are all just additional benefits to the refinement of mind and the sheer fun that comes when a master is deploying his or her advanced skills.

One of the biggest obstacles that comes to mind is the need to justify the time spent on practice. When our perspective is short-sighted it's natural to think that spending an hour a day practicing one little technique over and over is a poor use of time. The strange paradox is, though, that practicing in such a way actually seems to create time rather than consume time. If the practice session is carried out with intense focus, the mind seems to become refined and more efficient. After an intensely focused morning practice session, the rest of the day feels longer than it would normally be, and the work that you had planned seems to get done in a fraction of its usual time. As Jon Kabat-Zinn says, the answer to having either too much time, or not enough time, is meditation.

Not only is it often an illusion that a morning practice session will eat up your time, but also, it is an illusion that daily practice sessions will make for a boring life. During the practice session you may experience boredom, but the coinciding refinement of mind will decrease the overall boredom throughout the remainder of the day because the mind itself is being sharpened. When the mind has been sharpened in such a way, thoughts become more interesting and the senses tend to have more clarity. So, if you have decided that the skill you have in mind will be beneficial enough in the long term, then spending an hour a day on practice drills that will develop that skill may be easily justifiable.

To drive the motivation to practice home some more, it's helpful to communicate to yourself what the consequences of *not* practicing are. Writing them down on a single page in point form and reviewing this list of consequences when motivation is sliding can be an effective way to find energy for practice. For example, a consequence of not practicing that is common to all people is that if they never develop mastery in any craft, they will have no choice but to be entertained almost purely by chemicals or by the media, perceiving everything in life as commercial culture delivers it to them. They will have no other means of escaping boredom and they will likely become a workaholic—regardless of whether they care for the job they find themselves in—simply for the sake of escaping their own head.

Taking a long-term perspective and visualizing the benefits of mastery can be an effective way to increase motivation also. Here, it is important to emphasize the connection between the daily practice session and the long-term outcome by meditating on this. The mind is a bit like a garden in that the work and nutrition you put into it grows into something later on. So, if you want to be motivated to practice in the morning, spend some time the evening before using visualization to reinforce that connection between daily practice and the long-term outcome.

My mind is a garden,

My thoughts are the seeds,

I can plant flowers,

Or I can plant weeds

—Anonymous

Another important factor in maintaining motivation is to regularly receive positive feedback. Celebrating early wins is crucial. Without these little breakthroughs along the way, the energy to push on will fade. A coach or mentor can be useful in delivering positive feedback for some art forms. However, if the activity is being practiced in privacy, like the early stages of developing songwriting skills, for example, some sort of partner may better be able to provide effective feedback. For example, a songwriter could develop alongside a co-writer or band members. Likewise, an aspiring author could join a writer's club to receive both constructive criticism and positive feedback.

Finally, when you feel you have been pushed to your absolute limits, sometimes the best approach is to take a break. Go do something else for a week, a month, or maybe longer, and return with a fresh perspective. It's incredible what the unconscious mind can sort out on its own.

How to Practice

There is a common myth that the longer a person keeps at something, the better they will get at it. That actually isn't true. In reality, if the activity is not practiced in a challenging and focused way that's deliberately designed to overcome weaknesses and improve upon strengths, the person's skills will atrophy and their abilities will suffer as a result of the formation of bad habits and of a weakening focus. In general, they will get worse over time. Evidence of this can be seen in older rock stars, for example. Not everybody becomes as proficient as Tommy Emmanuel at guitar playing after decades of playing professionally. Those rockers who play a simple, straight-forward rhythm guitar style, never develop more fluent skills unless they work towards it deliberately. In fact, many of them develop a sloppy technique over time that is less effective than the technique they had in their earlier years.

For skills to progress the art form needs to be broken into its elements, and exercises designed, that will challenge the apprentice to refine his or her skills. Designing exercises effectively is a large part of the challenge toward mastery. The more effectively an exercise hones a particular skill, the more fluent the apprentice will become.

Starting the Fire

"I fear not the man who has practiced 10,000 kicks once, but I fear the man who has practiced one kick 10,000 times."[22]

—Bruce Lee

If an aspiring musician wants to learn to play an advanced piece of music fluently and so practices the piece from start to finish over and over again, that musician will never reach fluency. No matter how many hours of practice he or she puts in in this way, the body-mind will never learn to play the piece fluently because it can't possibly know exactly what it needs to learn. This is where focus becomes extremely important. It is crucial that the apprentice or her coach design exercises that respect the limits of the body's ability to learn.

The effective way for the musician to learn the piece would be to first design exercises that focus on developing the techniques used within the song and once those techniques have been mastered, the musician would then learn the song in small chunks of perhaps a line or a couple bars at a time so that the body is able to become aware of what it needs to learn. If the musician attempts to learn the entire song at once, the body will never form a clear awareness of what exactly the musician is attempting to do.

The length of the practice sessions is important too. A useful analogy is to think of learning skills like starting a fire by rubbing two sticks together; If you keep stopping to rest, you won't ever build enough heat to start the fire. Likewise, if the practice sessions are too short, the body will not develop enough familiarity with the exercise and so the neural networks will never form. On the flip-side, if the sessions are too long, focus will wither and the practice session will become ineffective. For this reason, it is *generally* advised in performance psychology not to have sessions exceed one hour in length without a rest period.

Overall, mastery is attained by beginning with the basic skills that act as foundational skills for more advanced skills to be built upon. Exercises are designed that focus on developing proficiency at those foundational skills. Then further exercises are designed to develop nuances and styling. One of the most important parts of the mastery process is the design of such exercises that lead to unique style and character in the art form. The ability to design those exercises that develop the subtler techniques within an art form will come only when the apprentice's understanding of the art form has reached an advanced level.

Reaching Integrity

When observing the works of artists, or the performances of athletes, it's apparent that a small minority of people display a level of integrity that far exceeds the average within their field. In some cases, even the second best in the field appears to be significantly less skilled than the very best. However, adhering to my point of view stated earlier, I would like to suggest that this impressive display of integrity is not the result of innate genius but is instead the result of the master having set the bar high and having done what was required to reach that bar. The master artist reaches integrity by way of the following five elements:

- Effective Questioning

- Effective Materials

- Deep Understanding

- Intensely Focused and Well-Designed Practice

- Determination and Perseverance

The 'questioning' here involves both mentor questioning and self-questioning. By self-questioning, I mean examining the works of those who have come before and simply asking questions like 'How did they do that?' Then the artist investigates this either by thinking it through themselves or by finding the right materials to provide the answers. For example, an aspiring scientist will use top quality books, courses and mentors as her materials. As Tim Ferriss mentions in his book on skill mastery, *The Four-Hour Chef*, the right choice of materials is of extreme importance: With the right materials, a person can save years of what might otherwise have been wasted time on the road to mastery. With the wrong materials, they may never get there at all.[23]

To return to the example of songwriting, songwriters are influenced by an array of earlier songwriters (one of their learning materials) and their own songwriting tends to be a fusion of the elements of those influences. With a poor choice of influences, the result could have been some pretty awful music. But with a well-chosen set of influences, the resulting music may be incredible — if it is composed tastefully.

By starting with effective materials (e.g. mentors, books, courses, manuals) and asking effective questions, with focus and a mindset for integrity, a deep level of understanding can be reached. Then, as described above, the aspiring master develops a cleverly designed progressive plan, which he or she practices with intense focus until the desired integrity is arrived at.

Intricacy is not necessarily the aim. It can be the simpler activities that are the most enjoyable and the most effective too. But the simple activity is far more enjoyable and effective if it is performed fluently. For example, playing an intricate musical piece may not be as enjoyable or emotionally moving as a simpler one. And at the same time — the simplest music is far more effective when played passionately by somebody who is fluent than when played by a beginner. It can be good to have intricate skills but it's not necessarily effective to deploy them in most situations.

It's important to remember also that most world-class artists and other esteemed professionals are only showing you their best work. The renowned songwriting teacher, Pat Pattison, has a saying — *"Crap is the best fertilizer."*[24] Or, as he puts it elsewhere, *"Ninety percent of what you write is not your best ten percent."* For every song a professional songwriter releases, you can guarantee she's written at least ten more (usually hundreds more) that were basically crap. Even many of the most popular songwriters only have a small handful of extraordinarily good songs in their entire career. Writing a classic clearly isn't something they can do at conscious will.

Crap is the best fertilizer — it would be difficult to find any pursuit that this doesn't apply to. I'll remember it always.

Some Thoughts on Mentors

Having access to the right mentor can save years of what might have been wasted energy. A skilled mentor can point out to you where the common wastes of time are and how you can train most effectively. I have often found that by talking to a knowledgeable person for just one hour face-to-face, I am able to learn as much as I had learned in a year of formal education or of reading books on a subject. I walk away from a conversation like that thinking, 'Damn, I wish I knew all that five years ago.' Conversation can get to the heart of a matter very quickly and directly.

A further benefit to having a face-to-face mentor is that by spending a large amount of time around them, to some extent you can absorb some of their attitudes and skills in a way that greatly enhances progression toward mastery. There is also more social motivation involved with direct contact with the mentor. Our strong drive to fit in as human beings comes in handy in this case, as we learn more readily and quickly when immersed in a world full of people of integrity.

In areas where innovation or unique expression are a key goal, it's important to use various mentors over the course of your apprenticeship. A self-designed apprenticeship can be designed from early on and updated as your understanding deepens. In designing the apprenticeship, it is effective to decide what things you do like and what things you don't like about each particular mentor's work. Idolizing a mentor as if he or she were flawless will be the death of innovation as it will lead to becoming a superficial imitation of the idolized master. It's best to let go of any hero-worshipping attachment and to be honest with yourself about what you do and what you don't like in his or her work. If the work is impressive, break it down into what it's made up of. Determine what it is that contributes to that impressive effect that the work has. The whole is greater than the sum of the parts, so by looking at the parts separately we can often bring the initial impression of the work down to earth and see a little more clearly and with less attachment. By doing so, it becomes easier to determine which parts of the master's work you really do want to incorporate into your own work and which parts you don't. This will save an enormous amount of time and energy as you will not waste time attempting to learn every skill of the master in an attempt to imitate a style that has already been conquered. When you have removed the parts that don't inspire you, fill their place with elements of another mentor's work or your own innovations or something from a totally different field. In this way, a new *whole* is created that, as with the other artists' work, is greater than the sum of its parts.

Foundations of The Flow State

Relaxation and Homeostasis

To wing your course along the middle air;

If low, the surges wet your flagging plumes;

If high, the sun the melting wax consumes

—Daedalus to Icarus

"I had become a bona fide substance abuser. I had no idea that in taking this path, I was robbing myself of the stress hardiness people develop naturally in life."[25]

—George Mumford, The Mindful Athlete

The nervous system is never in a fixed state. Instead, it operates more like a thermostat, always fluctuating. In terms of energy levels, the nervous system swings through waves from low to high, to some degree, depending on many factors. And the higher I go, the lower I must go. How else could the body and mind maintain equilibrium?

This tendency for bodily systems to maintain a healthy balance is known scientifically as homeostasis.[1] In the central nervous system, the trouble with a wide homeostatic swing is that the mind is more turbulent and deluded when its energy level swings far from the middle. So, to function with a clear mind, it's necessary to learn to reduce the homeostatic swing so that the energy level is rising and falling in small waves either side of the middle. Or in other words — mental relaxation is a key aspect of high performance.

---

[1] *Homeostasis; any self-regulating process by which biological systems tend to maintain stability while adjusting to conditions that are optimal for survival. If homeostasis is successful, life continues; if unsuccessful, disaster and death ensues. The stability attained is actually a dynamic equilibrium, in which continuous change occurs yet relatively uniform conditions prevail. (2017) from www.britannica.com/science/homeostasis*

The homeostatic swing can be reduced through relaxation practices, an improved diet, and through changes in our thinking, our belief system, and our external environment. Over time, this lower level of stimulation turns from an experience of boredom to one of serenity. The serene state that we call *flow* is much more likely to occur in a mentally relaxed state.

Enjoying serenity doesn't mean avoiding having fun. In fact, it's much easier to have fun and to *genuinely* enjoy it when the body and mind are conditioned toward a more relaxed physiology. But without relaxation personal growth will be muted. It's a scientific fact that neurogenesis — the formation of new neurons — is stunted when a person is either depressed or over stimulated by anxiety.

As for boredom, the famous Holocaust survivor, Alice Herz Sommers, held the belief that boredom is the worst thing a person can endure in life. If a Holocaust survivor thinks that about boredom, then that explains a lot about human behavior in general. But why do people fear boredom so much?

Maybe it's that the untamed mind becomes most turbulent when there is a lack of external stimulation, as the mind creates drama to support the habitual fluctuations of the nervous system. If the nervous system is used to swinging very high and low due to external stimulation from diet, dangerous situations etc., then when those stimulants are no longer present, the mind creates drama to coincide with the homeostatic swing that, out of habit, the nervous system is still following. This is why the mind tends to be clearer when the body is in a relaxed physiological state. There is less dramatizing (a.k.a. adrenalizing) and less distortion of perception.

The further we live from a relaxed homeostasis, the more we will go through life as victims of the conceptualizing mind: a turbulent mind that creates drama in the form of false perceptions and through stories that are not real. When the nervous system is agitated we miss the subtlest nudges that the body and unconscious mind send to alert us when something is off. And in this way, mental turbulence sucks sincerity and insight from the artist's works and reduces effectiveness. Not to mention, the way that out-of-sync nervous agitation removes our capacity to experience flow.

Small Things

"With free-soloing, obviously I know that I'm in danger, but feeling fearful while I'm up there is not helping me in any way. It's only hindering my performance, so I just set it aside and leave it be."[26]

—Alex Honnold referring to his record breaking free-solo climb of El Capitan wall (no ropes)

Cats are known for their ability to pounce with impressive speed but if you have ever watched or played with a cat you'll notice that they're never tense. And likewise, when a martial artist strikes a punch he keeps as loose as possible during the movement, only tightening his muscles upon impact. This allows him to deliver a powerful blow as he is able to move at maximum speed before making his body become rigid upon impact. The importance of relaxation is evident in almost every activity. A musician plays best when relaxed. A singer sings poorly if she over-tightens. Sparks of creativity happen when we are most relaxed. And so, it's clear that the body and mind function optimally when relaxed.

If I stand on a hot rock in the sun, I will feel a burning under my feet. If I listen to that pain, then I will immediately move to a shadier spot where my feet will not be blistered by the heat. But if I ignore the pain, the pain will increase over time as the heat builds and my body attempts to communicate the urgency with which I should move to avoid injury. In this way, the body gives subtle signals that are urging us to take action in order to keep safe or to maintain our health. If a person was to ignore those subtle signals, then the signals would need to get stronger until the person takes action, or until the person does change their perception of that which is plaguing their mind. Likewise, in the moment of creating an art work, an artist is monitoring her inner-state while the unconscious gives nudges to steer the artist's actions. A songwriter feels off when she has gone to an unsuitable chord that does not express her true feelings. Then she feels relaxed and at home as she finds the chord that hits the spot.

Have you ever been looking for something at the grocery store, but couldn't find what you were looking for despite the fact that it was directly in front of your face? In observing those moments, we notice that the reason why we don't see it is because we unconsciously exclude certain possibilities from our search. You may have been thinking it could be anywhere but directly in front of your face, because you had already decided it would be hard to find. Or you may have decided that the object you were looking for would be a little larger than it really was.

Our emotions seem to be subject to this same effect. If we are always looking for big, strong emotions to drive our actions, then we will ignore the subtler ones. The outcome of this way of living is that the nervous system will habitually produce a more turbulent homeostatic swing and then the distortion of our perceptions follows.

The same goes for thoughts or ideas. We never really think up an idea consciously. Ideas are formed unconsciously and presented to the conscious mind. If I am always looking for big ideas, then I will miss all the smaller ones. But haven't you ever had a problem that stumped you for years, and when you looked back at it later you realized you could have ended it the day it started, if only you had thought of that simple little action that you eventually took to fix it? So, it's often the little ideas that are actually the most effective, yet those are the ideas that we may be missing out on if we're always searching for big things. The subtleties of the art form may be neglected — as well as many potentially effective ideas — if the artist is looking only for something big.

The Relationship Between Relaxation and Concentration

Imagine you are sitting at night under a fluorescent light with a broken ballast. The faulty light flickers on for a second, then off again, continuously as you are attempting to read a challenging book. What are your chances of actually comprehending the reading material under this interrupted light source? It would be tricky. But with a steady stream of light you would have had a far better chance at understanding the material.

Attention functions in much the same way as the flickering light. Many people who've never tried meditation don't realize how short our natural single-pointed attention span really is. If asked how long they can maintain attention for, they often think something along the lines of, 'Well I've watched movies that go for three hours straight so I would guess around three hours.' If they try meditation however, they will find that even to hold perfectly uninterrupted, single-pointed attention for just a few seconds is very difficult. It becomes evident that there is a stream of thoughts passing through the mind as attention flips back and forth between the object of focus and that which distracts the mind.

In this way, we are constantly operating with our performance being limited in the same way as the faulty flickering light would limit our understanding of that challenging book. When trying to understand phenomena, our comprehension is constantly being limited by the length of our single-pointed attention span. We see the world in a distorted manner as a result of this superficial lack in understanding. Our depth of understanding in any area has been stunted by the limits of our attention span.

Thankfully, there are ways that our attention span can be cultivated to allow for better mental functioning. Even a split-second improvement in a single-pointed attention span makes a noticeable difference in the quality and depth of thoughts. This also leads to the mere action of thinking becoming much more interesting and enjoyable in itself.

In ancient times, the people of Asia developed meditation techniques that enhance various qualities of mind. Perhaps the most effective of those for developing attention span is the Buddhist practice of *Shamatha* meditation.

Much of the literature on meditation is full of dogmatic folklore, but in recent times meditation has been studied extensively by scientists and has been found to be very effective in many ways.[2] The gist of Shamatha meditation is that if you want to better your understanding of phenomena, and if you want to improve the quality of everything you do, then start by developing your attention span. And to do this, the first step is to master the art of relaxed focus.

Without relaxation, the mind becomes turbulent and cannot stay on a chosen object. Attention cannot be voluntarily sustained if the mind is over-excited. But it's not enough to simply reduce excitation. Reducing excitation too far will only lead to mental laxity or even sleepiness and the mind will wander again. So, sustained focus requires *alertness* and this can be achieved only if the physiological energy can be maintained in the middle (that is, if the mind is not too relaxed, nor too excited).

---

[2] *For further information see, for example, books by the Mind and Life institute in California such as Destructive Emotions: A Scientific Dialogue with the Dalai Lama, (2004): Bantam*

Maintaining attention is a skill that can be garnered through practice.

Having experimented with Shamatha meditation myself, I have become familiar with some of the benefits. I have found too, that many of those same benefits can also be achieved through simple, focused practice drills, such as those that are encountered in the practice of an art form or sport. I believe this is partly why the development of a skill can make the flow state occur more often. The practice drills and the challenge to maintain relaxed focus — which the pursuit of mastery provides — can lead to such enjoyment.

Patience

One of the most important lessons we can learn through the pursuit of mastery is the necessity of having patience. Some skills will appear to be impossible to master at first but with a continuously patient approach, the apprentice finds that what once appeared insurmountable becomes effortlessly easy. This lesson can then be applied to other areas of life and can increase a person's confidence in the face of uncertainty or initial defeat. In Eastern philosophy, patience is defined not merely by begrudgingly enduring misfortune, but by the continuous acceptance of what is. To be patient requires sitting with uncertainty and its coinciding discomfort as we progress through those awkward stages on the road to mastery. It is here that the growth mindset is so crucial. By viewing ourselves as ever-changing rather than as fixed entities we are able to see that change is possible. Otherwise we are stuck with the self we know. The one that can't write the song. The one that can't hit the archery target. And so on.

It is important also, not to race ahead when learning skills. There are many skills that require weeks or even years of preparation before they are even attempted. It is said in the field of musicianship that if the musician does not first learn to relax with and enjoy playing her instrument, she will never develop the ability to hit people in the heart with her music. I have seen this in many advanced musicians who hooked onto a rigorous plan for developing impressive skills right from the beginning. They developed incredible technical skills but their playing always seemed so contrived. Nobody was moved by their music. Not even themselves.

There is a parallel to this notion in the practice of shamatha meditation mentioned earlier. It is said that to progress with shamatha meditation it's necessary to first develop relaxation, then concentration, then vividity. As discussed earlier, concentration cannot develop without the skill of relaxation. And a vivid mind that is not tamed by relaxed concentration will be very turbulent and unwieldy.

Beginner's Mind and the Symbolic Mental Image

"An open, "beginner's" mind allows us to be receptive to new possibilities and prevents us from getting stuck in the rut of our own expertise, which often thinks it knows more than it does ... Are you able to see the sky, the stars, the trees and the water and the stones, and really see them as they are right now with a clear and uncluttered mind? Or are you actually seeing them through the veil of your own thoughts and opinions?"[27]

—Jon Kabat-Zinn

"The mind of the beginner is empty, free of the habits of the expert, ready to accept, to doubt, and open to all possibilities."[28]

—Zen Master, Shunryu Suzuki

A young child attends an airshow with his father. Since he rarely spends time with his father, the day out is a very special occasion for him which he thoroughly enjoys. Hearing about the child's newfound enthusiasm for airshows, his school teachers suggest that since he's good at math and likes airshows he should become an aerospace engineer. When the child eventually does become an engineer however, he finds that life as an engineer feels nothing like he had dreamt. Although unaware of it, he had connected the feeling of being with his father at the airshow, with the thought of himself as an engineer and had been led toward a career for which he had no genuine interest.

This is a very common mistake that people make in many decisions as we often, in modern life at least, are required to make decisions in such a way. Images are tied with feelings. Those images are supposed to represent livable realities, such as the experience of achieving a particular goal. But, while dreaming, we ourselves have imbued those images with those qualities, and the realities that they are supposed to represent may turn out to be very different to what we have imagined.

We make the same mistake in relating to the scenes that play out in the mind. When anticipating an argument, for example, there is a tendency to rehearse the situation in blown-out proportion. This rehearsal of the argument distorts our perception of the other person. When we next see them, there can often be a negative aura about them, but in some cases, it may simply be our own projection. What we think, observe and believe today, affects tomorrow's perception.

We see the world around us all colored up in this way. Tainted, you could say, by past experience. Distorted, by fear. But how does it look when we see it all with fresh eyes? To look at the world around us that we feel we've known for years from a fresh perspective, as it is today, without projecting past associations upon it? There is a translucent shield between our eyes and the world, coloring what we see. To drop the shield would require a certain level of humility. It takes courage to see things as they really are.

To see things as they are with fresh eyes, and with an unassuming mindset as if you are a novice, is known in Zen as "beginner's mind". If a painter picks up her brush each time with a sense of mystery, not assuming she knows all there is to be found in the canvas already, then she is coming to the canvas with a spirit of curiosity and a childlike playfulness. In this way, she is likely to discover unique ways of doing things rather than falling into the groove of her old habits. The practice of beginner's mind is another mindset that will benefit not only to the artist's work but all other aspects of the

artist's life as well.

Non-Striving

"In the meditative domain, the best way to achieve your own goals is to back off from striving for results and instead to start focusing carefully on seeing and accepting things as they are, moment by moment. With patience and regular practice, movement toward your goals will take place by itself."[29]

—Jon Kabat-Zinn

Keeping Up with the Joneses: The Game of One-Up-Manship

When we want to impress other people, we become easily impressed *by* other people. The more we desire a particular trait, the more we worship the person who has that trait. In extreme cases, the person begins to appear as being elevated, out of reach and otherworldly. From that position, they can easily make further impression on us

— thus the desire to impress renders us —

impressionable.

I don't believe that people think it's their job in life to be productive. More accurately, I believe, that in the back of their minds, they are under the false belief that it's their job to be impressive. And this notion where a person believes they have to be impressive not only creates a lot of struggles within but also creates many problems in the world at large. A lot of the negative side of modern culture has come out of this underlying motive.

In the pursuit of mastery, if the artist's motivation is to make his work ultimately impressive and he cannot bear to release it until it is utterly perfected or at its ultimate impressiveness, then when will that time ever come? It can go on and on infinitely. Like an internal drug, the desire to impress is an obsession. And what would really come of it anyway? Do people even *want* to be impressed? How does the outcome change if the focus is shifted to *inspiration* rather than impression?

As in the words of 'The Ice Man', Wim Hof, "It's not ego, it's *we go!*" True artistry is about expressing the beauty that's in all of us, not about climbing to alpha status in a display of athleticism or cleverness. The game of one-up-manship, when taken to the extreme, does not only create ineffective work but also hinders progression and prevents enjoyment of the artwork itself.

It becomes clear while practicing meditation that bliss never comes when you are striving for it. Likewise, when the desire to impress is not present, the mind is calmer, warmer and clearer. Living without the game of one-up-manship leads us along a certain path in life as our daily decisions will be different to what they would be otherwise. This accumulates over the years to a life lived with greater enjoyment and is likely to have a better outcome. In contrast, a life lived with a constant desire to impress is likely to be full of regret. This transfers to the pursuit of mastery in any endeavor, be it business, art, sport or science. A work that is born out of the need for admiration is going to have a less inspiring outcome than one that is born of sincerity. Many people seem to have a sixth sense for sincerity in art. When they are truly interested in sincerity they spot the posers.

Non-Striving

"If, while washing dishes, we think only of the cup of tea that awaits us, thus hurrying to get the dishes out of the way as if they were a nuisance... we are not alive during the time we are washing the dishes. In fact, we are completely incapable of realizing the miracle of life while standing at the sink. If we can't wash the dishes, chances are we won't be able to drink our tea either. While drinking the cup of tea, we will be thinking of other things, barely aware of the cup in our hands. Thus, we are sucked away into the future — and we are incapable of actually living one minute of life."[30]

—Thich Nhat Hanh, Vietnamese Buddhist monk and poet

When we are on the road to mastery it is important that we set goals, and create habits with an end in mind, but when it comes to the actual moment of the practice itself, it may be best not to strive for results at all. Not only is performance best when the activity is an end in itself, but even a practice session is best approached in this way– with a spirit of non-striving. Just as Thich Nhat Hanh says, wash the dishes to wash the dishes, so too, we are better off to practice for the enjoyment of the practice itself.

This is a key principle for long-term perseverance toward mastery as well as for short-term enjoyment. By practicing with a spirit of 'non-striving', we are practicing the non-striving mindset in a way that will transfer to the other activities during the day. It would be a dull experience to go through life always focused on reaping rewards.

So, in the moment of practice or performance of the art form it is extremely beneficial to approach with a spirit of playful investigation, enjoying the practice for itself. This way the improvement will still come but only as a byproduct of the practice. There are times on the road to mastery when we need to stop and plan ahead with an end in mind but this mindset can be dropped during practice sessions and during performance. As in the spirit of meditation.

Open Awareness

> *"A brain in doubt, leaves it out"*
>
> —John Whitfield, on motion-induced blindness

For performance to be optimized, it's important to be seeing things as they are — being aware of what is really happening without distorting or ignoring those aspects that are not desirable. But in our artistry, and in all areas of life, through our tendency to compare the reality to the ideal, we distort our perception of what's really happening. By casting comparisons in such a way, we are clouding our awareness of what's really happening. If you are skeptical about this, then I recommend viewing video demonstrations of "motion-induced blindness". In motion-induced blindness an object can seem to disappear completely, right before the viewer's eyes, when in fact it remained right where it was all along. This unconscious editing may be happening very often in all activities we are involved with.

Through the practice of open awareness (a.k.a. choiceless awareness), a person begins to realize that they are constantly categorizing and judging. Things are often shunned as being "bad" or praised as being "good". Not necessarily in those words, but there is a felt sense of wrongness or rightness about things. To see things in such a way is not clear perception. It is a distorted version of reality in which everything is perceived in relation to rules and formulas, likes and dislikes. Conforming to the "right" way of doing things can lead to a loss of beauty and of free-expression in the art form.

Even in sports, judgement can decrease performance as the player becomes overly rigid and attempts to force his body to repeat the desired pattern of movement, the "right" way, rather than to trust his body to adapt spontaneously to the moment.

In the judging mind, we see events as good (liked), bad (disliked) and neutral. The stuff we don't want to see or know about is thought to be 'bad' and therefore we conveniently shun it and consequently lose awareness of it as it escapes the conscious mind. What we consider to be 'neutral' we consider to be unimportant and so we ignore it and it slips out of our conscious awareness. The things we desire, we think of as 'good', and so we try hard to focus on them and to repeat their occurrence. Focus then becomes too narrow and awareness of the full reality in front of us is lost. Progress is stagnated in all three of these scenarios.

In artistry, it's important to have a clear image of the desired outcome and to be aware of how closely the performance matches up with that intention. But what is not effective, is to ignore what is undesirable. If the unwanted aspects are ignored, the ability for the conscious and unconscious to cooperate effectively is limited. Alternatively, if things are seen in open awareness, then the unconscious processes have the opportunity to learn from, or respond to that input. But if the full version of reality is edited by the exclusion of undesirable aspects, then the unconscious mind will never receive the full version of the information and so the learning process will be stunted.

In the optimal learning experience, by seeing things without judgement, we are seeing what is happening rather than 'how well' or 'how badly' it's happening. The mind is at its most effective when perception is 'non-dual'. Or in other words, when what we are interested in is occupying our *whole* field of awareness. To look for how well or how badly something is happening would dissipate energy by creating a duality. The focus can't really be *fully* on what *is happening* if the mind is simultaneously computing *how well* it's happening. In such a scenario, a part of the mental processing power is being used for the operation of measuring performance.

One more note — when you begin to notice that you are excluding and judging elements of the field of perception as described, it can be impulsive to judge the judging itself. It is a bit of a kick to the ego when we notice that we have this tendency to be so precious that we need to shut things out. But to judge the judging itself would just reinforce the same process all over again. So, it's best just to let the judging, categorizing and exclusion fall away on its own in the light of awareness.

Detachment from the Master Identity

In Borneo, there is a very unusual way of catching monkeys. A banana is placed inside a trap with a small hole in it that is just big enough for a monkey to fit its hand through. When the monkey discovers the food, it squeezes its hand into the trap and grasps the banana. While the monkey's hand is clenched, however, the hand forms a wider shape and so it can no longer fit back through the hole. As the hunter approaches the monkey to capture it, the monkey is terrified and tries to pull away. All the monkey would have to do is let go of the food and it could easily escape, but it's too attached to its objective to see this. And so, the monkey is easily captured as a consequence of its refusal to let go.

We hear this story and at first think how silly the monkey must be, to hold on to something when the consequences are so high. But, we are actually doing much the same thing by holding on to our thoughts, opinions, attitudes, perceptions, identities and obsessions. Too often, we hold on to our conditions and our limiting beliefs simply because we have either built up an identity around them or because we have become comfortable with the way things have been. So much could be gained from breaking that inertia and letting go. From stepping outside our comfort zone, and journeying into the unknown. To do this requires riding with insecurity, not knowing for sure how things will turn out. But as the renowned social worker and author Virginia Satir says, *"Many people prefer the certainty of misery over the misery of uncertainty."*

One of the major obstacles that stands in the way of us letting go of the hypothetical banana is simply that, just like the monkey, we are most often unaware that we are holding on and that there were other options on the plate. But the thing is that the alternative options don't come into awareness until after the letting go happens. And the letting go does not occur until the holding on is brought to our attention.

If we take notice of what holding on feels like, and likewise, of what letting go feels like, then by questioning ourselves — "What am I holding on to that is limiting me?" for example--often the limiting belief will be brought into awareness. Though it can take a lot of time if you are holding on to that banana too tightly.

In our pursuit of mastery, there are many situations where letting go would be the most effective action. Many people mistake obsession for sincere dedication. Amongst musicians for example, many people believe that a "real musician" has to be pursuing music exclusively. That music must be his life. But it has often been said by well-known songwriters that one of the best pieces of advice for improving your songwriting is to go and get busy doing something else. They say — "Get away from music so that you'll have something to write about. Don't be one of those songwriters who writes songs about songwriting. Who can relate to that?"

When pursuing mastery of a craft, it's very easy to get caught up in memorizing knowledge and perfecting techniques so obsessively that the fundamental goal is put off or even never attempted at all. For example, guitarists with advanced technical skills are far more common than guitarists who can write well. But most of those advanced guitarists have been dreaming all along of writing. They are clinging to what they know well and are afraid to let go and endure the awkwardness of starting something new — being a beginner at writing. Having advanced skills can be very rewarding and a worthwhile goal to pursue, but when it becomes an addiction, then it is no longer about the sincere effect of the art form (communication through music, for example). When it becomes an obsession, it's just an attempt to bulletproof oneself as a solid master of the craft.

Holding on to the 'master identity' is a limiting mindset. As mentioned earlier, one of the key practices for innovation is to play around without fear. If you are afraid to make mistakes you will not try anything new. And if your self-worth rests on your identity as an artist, you will have a lot to fear. A lot of very innovative art works have been created by people who were pursuing the art form for fun rather than doing it to 'be something'. If the goal of the artist is to 'be something', then the artwork is a means to an end and that stands in the way of enjoyment.

Effortless Action

"Leave no trace"

—Buddhist proverb

We live in a society full of fierce competition. When a person is lagging behind we say, "try harder!" It seems obvious that if laziness causes us to fall behind, then trying hard must cause us to succeed. But in this way of thinking we have neglected the fact that the opposite extreme is just as problematic. When a person tries *too hard*, not only do they burn out in the long term but the quality of what they do in the meantime is also reduced. When a person tries too hard they become tense and rigid. The athlete over tightens and seizes up; the artist loses touch with the unconscious processes and forces out an ugly piece; the wood craftsman's work is shonky. That relaxed concentration we experience in the flow state is not reached through force.

In the pursuit of mastery, we observe over and over again how trying too hard cripples performance. So why do we persist? It's like the monkey with the banana in his hand mentioned earlier. We won't let go. We are attached to the idea that with our conscious mind we can control things and take credit for having produced the outcome. But perhaps, we should be no prouder of the outcome than a gardener is of his fruit. The gardener has put in a lot of work to set up the conditions that lead to the production of beautiful fruit. But he did not invent fruit. Nor did he shape it or create any of its other qualities. He can be proud of the work he put into the process of growing, but beyond that he can only stand in wonder at the fruit itself. He cannot take full credit for its beauty.

It's our desire to gain credit for the outcome that keeps us from fully acknowledging the abilities of the unconscious processes. Instead, we would do better to build trust in the unconscious processes, our instincts, natural sensitivity, reflexes we've built through training etc. As that trust builds, the body and mind are freed to perform optimally.

It seems, there is a time for conscious effort and a time for letting go to instinct. During the preparation stage we plan things through, we visualize, we practice with presence. Then, in the execution of the art form, we let go and enter the flow state. The instincts we have built up during the preparation stage have been growing over time and they may have a surprise in store. Our performance can sometimes be hindered by interfering with this instinct — by assuming we know better. There is an aspect of humility involved with high performance.

But we can be fools to think we've got the right mindset if we simply *try* to relax. Trying to relax is just another form of trying. It is *'trying not to try'*. It may be better to approach this with the mindset of *letting* it happen. To formulate a clear representation of the desired outcome and encourage it rather than pushing it. To ask that unconscious intelligence for the desired outcome and remain open to the unknown.

So where is the line between trying too hard and not hard enough? As is commonly observed, one instruction given to a dozen different people carries with it a dozen different meanings. Words are very limited in what they can do and so we could never formulate 'how to approach action' as an instruction. A person needs to discover for themselves what it means to act without getting in their own way.

Acceptance

"Once we accept our limits, we go beyond them."

—Albert Einstein

Acceptance means to see things as they really are, without distortion. Too often, we add or subtract from what is really there before our eyes. In artistry, this distortion deprives our work of beauty.

To accept a weakness in our craftsmanship is a different thing to justifying it. There is no need to justify a weakness but at the same time it's important that the artist can *accept* weaknesses. When we cannot accept our weaknesses, we hide them from ourselves. Passing under the radar of our awareness, our weaknesses go on unnoticed. For this reason, it's important to be able to admit to weaknesses with full acceptance. If you can accept it, then you can see it. If you can see it, then you are aware of it, and only then might it change. If a person is not accepting his or her own weaknesses, then they are holding on to the belief that they are already better than they are. But there is a contradiction in this. How can a person be better right now than they are right now?

When we begin to accept our errors, our poor technique, our weaknesses, at first it seems as though they have become exacerbated and that, by letting go of control, we have become worse at performing the activity. But what is actually happening is that we have become more aware of the weaknesses that we were not seeing before. Our performance has not really become worse at all. The illusion that we have become worse leads us to try harder to gain control and that then fuels a struggle in which we tense up and then the problems *really are* exacerbated.

The alternative is to accept things as they are. When we accept our weaknesses, sometimes an automatic process occurs in which the unconscious mind seems to effortlessly sort out ways to fix the problem. Answers come like brain mail. There is often no need to even attempt to fix the weakness. The improvement is a natural process that unfolds of its own accord.

Synergy

"The mundane in the miraculous and the

miraculous in the mundane."

—Buddhist proverb

In considering the pursuit of mastery there comes a time when we question if it's really worthwhile to go through the process at all when so much time on the road to mastery will be spent doing things that seem very mundane. But it is one of the central observations in Eastern philosophy that a lot of our mental anguish in life stems from our tendency to mistake the part for the whole.

This is particularly true when it comes to boredom. When people think that life is nothing but a boring mundane situation, they have mistaken a part of life for the whole of life. If all the most incredible moments that occur over a lifespan were to occur in the space of one week, it would be easy to see that life as a whole is far from mundane. The road to mastery can be seen from that same angle — as a whole it may be very worthwhile.

This tendency to mistake the part for the whole is also applicable to the artwork itself. For example, an artist could think, "Why should I bother to spend time practicing one little technique when it seems such a boring little thing? Is it really worth spending any time on at all?"

If we use water as an analogy — water is made up of hydrogen and oxygen but neither hydrogen, nor oxygen, bear the qualities of water on their own. The qualities of water are not merely the sum of the qualities of hydrogen plus the qualities of oxygen. In some way, new qualities are born when two or more elements are combined together.

As an artist, you can never know how things will turn out when you combine various elements. The missing ingredient could be the most unlikely thing. On its own it may be nothing extraordinary, but when combined with other elements a new whole is created with new qualities. In music, for example, there are many extraordinary rock bands that have not a single band member who is particularly extraordinary on their own.

Who knows what will happen when you add something to the mix. The quality of the whole can never be found in the parts. Nothing impressive is made up purely of impressive parts. And so, in the *learning* process, we break down the whole in order to learn from its less impressive parts in a down to earth manner. *But* in the *creation* of something new, we are constructing an effective whole using parts that may each be quite

mundane on their own.

Creativity

Introduction

"Creative thinking is not a talent, it is a skill that can be learned. It empowers people by adding strength to their natural abilities which improves teamwork, productivity and, where appropriate, profits."[31]

—Edward de Bono

Why do so many songwriters make incredibly good songs when they're young but then write such disappointing work later in life? And at the other end — why is it practically unheard of for a young kid to make brilliantly crafted songs? The reason is that creativity is a process rather than an innate character attribute. When we encounter beautiful works of art and clever inventions it's easy to be so captivated as to forget that behind their creation is years of learning and tinkering, trying and failing. What may be innate, is the creator's aesthetic sensitivity — her eye for style. But whether or not that tastefulness is a display of genius is merely a matter of opinion. There is a side to creativity that involves skill and that skill is not innate; it is developed through a long process.

One of the key attributes that leads to a better outcome in innovation is the ability to work through agonizing periods of uncertainty. Innovation happens more effectively when people work for longer at finding a solution. The need to appear quick-minded is the biggest killer of creativity. Those who are willing to tinker for longer are far more likely to produce a better outcome, all other conditions being equal.

The creative process requires the willingness to switch between what are often referred to as the 'open state' and the 'closed state'. In the open state, the innovator is considering all options no matter how absurd. There are no boundaries set in the open state. This is the time for trial and error, and a willingness to appear a little crazy. It is a time to let the mind roam freely before boundaries are selected to form the closed state.

The narrowing of boundaries in the closed state is a necessary part of the process as it eases mental processing. For example, if members of a rock band have no idea what sort of vibe they're going for, it will be difficult for them to get anything out at all. It is important to form questions, function-statements, etc. that set a clear guideline for the desired outcome. Otherwise, mental energy will be dissipated so much so, that realistically, the work will never be produced. Still, the function statement (or questions posed) should be left as open as possible in relation to the desired outcome to avoid prematurely constricting the options.

In the lifespan of the innovator, the creative process flows through an apprenticeship phase (be it a formal or informal apprenticeship), followed by a tinkering phase, then an incubation phase and finally, the insight comes.

The Apprenticeship Phase

During the apprenticeship phase the mind is primed for future innovation through the learning of skills and by developing a depth of understanding that allows the apprentice to navigate his field. He learns what has worked and what has not worked in that field. He learns which areas within that narrow field need solutions and thus finds areas within it to focus his energy on.

By developing a unique range of skills, the apprentice is much more likely to produce unique solutions in his attempts to tackle problems. Typically, in both science and art, innovations have been created through influence from other fields and, usually by mistake, through play. For example, Velcro was invented by George de Mestral, when he found he was getting burdock seeds (cobbler's pegs) stuck to his clothes while hiking. And in music, most fresh sounds are made by combining an unusual array of influences from different genres. The music of Mozart — who was actually a highly skilled billiard player — had been influenced partly by the click of billiard balls as they bounced around the table.

It should be added, also, that unique situations and unique relationships between people are important factors that often lead to innovation by providing unusual input and thus leading to unique ideas.

What is also important during the apprenticeship phase is that the aspiring innovator does not label himself prematurely, as that would stunt creativity by preventing the apprentice from ever applying his knowledge to other fields where it would provide fresh input.

The apprenticeship phase is about learning skills through intensive immersion within a field. That expertise is then complemented by input from other learning, which usually occurs during leisure time.

The apprenticeship phase forms the foundation for a productive tinkering phase.

The Tinkering Phase

It is in the tinkering phase that a deeper exploration takes place. This is where the innovator is venturing into the great unknown as he follows his curiosity. Where in the apprenticeship phase he was only venturing into territory that was unknown to himself, during the tinkering phase, he may be exploring what is unknown to humanity altogether. This requires a persistent acceptance of uncertainty. The innovator may ride with uncertainty in this way for years on end before he has anything to show for the time he has invested in the pursuit. The need for certainty is what prevents most people from ever doing anything particularly innovative in their lifetimes in any area of life. It seems we all have a deep fear of the unknown. But if we are to be innovative at all, we do need to take the plunge into the unknown. The need for certainty and to be doing what is already considered to be valid, puts a closed door on innovation.

During the tinkering phase, the innovator is not just tinkering physically with tools and works but also mentally with his perception of the situation. By loosening up his perception of what he's dealing with, the tinkerer is able to open his mind to receiving a vast array of ideas from the unconscious. For example, an innovative guitarist may see her guitar as a block of wood with strings across it. This way of seeing it opens up her perception of what a guitar is and how it should *or could* be played. In this way, the guitarist's perception of her instrument is freed from the constraints imposed by authority, knowledge and prestige.

The tinkering stage is the time to become aware of those prematurely defined limitations lingering in the back of the mind. These are uncovered through a process of experimentation and self-questioning.

The innovator provokes the arrival of new ideas and methods by turning things on their heads, playing with absurd possibilities and putting himself in strange situations. Even limitations themselves can lead to new possibilities. Some of the most unique music I've ever heard was created by people who refused to use anything but a single instrument to create an entire album. With limited resources, the innovator can be forced into a situation where he will focus purely on the fundamental aim. This, in some cases, can lead to simpler and more effective ways of doing things than having limitless possibilities ever would have.

In short, the tinkering phase of the creative process requires the courage to persevere through the discomfort of uncertainty and the potential for failure.

The innovator plays at solving the problem in an interplay between the conscious and the unconscious mind. Finally, when his intellect is exhausted, he gives up! Then, usually without knowing it, he has entered the incubation phase of the creative process.

The Incubation Phase

Self-doubt is an important and inevitable part of the creative process. In the incubation phase the innovator is coming to terms with the blow to his ego, which he has just endured. He wonders about the worthiness of his work. He is likely questioning whether it was even a worthwhile task to pursue to begin with. Having been defeated by the task, the innovator will often take up something new or go on a holiday to ease the stress of having failed at something so core to his identity. Unbeknown to the innovator, however, the creative process is still continuing. His holiday is a part of the process itself. It's often said in creative fields,

"If you want to solve a problem, get it away from your heart."

Since desire leads to distortion of perception, the innovator becomes like the monkey holding the banana. He clings so tightly to the aim that he cannot see the situation clearly. It's like looking at something with your eyes too close to it. Vision is obscured and the matter is not seen for what it is. From a further distance, however, the situation may be easier to navigate. And so, the intuitive leap may come when he least expects it, after he thought the task had been left to defeat.

Insight

When the insight finally comes, there remain two pitfalls

to be aware of. The first is that it may actually be wrong.

Faraday, Huxley, Darwin, Plank, Einstein and Poincare

have all said that flashes of intuitive insight can

sometimes be incorrect.[32] Einstein himself claimed he

lost two years of hard work to a false inspiration. Even if

the unconscious intelligence is unfathomably deep, I

think it's important to remember that we are interpreting

its expressions or signals with the very limited conscious

mind as our receiver.

The second pitfall is to *believe* that the insight is

wrong, or that it is invalid or too controversial to be

accepted. In many situations, an innovation will appear to

be so absurd that it will be disregarded by the innovator's

peers or even by the innovator himself. One of the

world's most esteemed scientists, V.S. Ramachandran, when questioned about the creative process he went through that led to unusual but effective treatments using mirrors to treat stroke sufferers and people with 'phantom limbs', responded by saying,

> I always tell my students, some of the most amazing discoveries have come from jokes. They started out as a joke […] The very idea of a mirror to treat one-sixth of mankind. One-sixth of mankind suffers a stroke. It's so outrageous, people would just discard it for that reason.[33]

Another excellent example of this is the famous story of when, in 1846, the Hungarian Doctor, Ignaz Semmelweis, first discovered that deaths due to puerperal fever could be dramatically reduced if the hospital staff washed their hands before delivering babies — he was ridiculed by his peers.[3] Fortunately, those thinkers both went ahead with the research despite that they would be seen as being crazy.

____

[3] *The Semmelweis Reflex was named after Ignaz Semmelweis to refer to peoples' tendency to have a reflex-like rejection of new knowledge that conflicts with current strongly held beliefs.*

Roadblocks to Mastery

Anger and Frustration

"Research finds that anger management therapies- like hitting pillows or other attempts at "catharsis" or "getting it all out" - increase rage, rather than decrease it [...] Expression isn't always necessary, contrary to popular belief."[34]

—Bruce Perry, M.D., PH.D., author of 'Born for Love'

Since frustration (or anger) is encountered so often on the road to mastery, a deep understanding of the nature and meaning of frustration is essential in the pursuit of mastery. But when we talk about anger or frustration, how do we know we are each talking about the same inner experience? An outward display of aggression is not always accompanied by the inner experience of anger. When attacking the ball during sport for example, the inner sensation may be completely different to that uncomfortable feeling that we experience when we're in the heat of an argument. And acts of "passive aggression" do not really involve any outward display of aggression at all, but we can infer that the person is experiencing anger internally when being passive aggressive.

An outward display of aggression is sometimes warranted and can be an effective action, but when it *is* the most suitable action, I am suggesting that it never carries with it the internal discomfort of what we can call "anger". The English language is very under-equipped when it comes to describing emotions. In some languages, such as the Tibetan language, there are hundreds of words for describing emotions and they each have very distinct meanings.

Before I describe my own view on anger, I would like to point out that I believe compassionately motivated aggression is actually one of the most *under*-employed actions of all in everyday life. In short — in this culture at least — we are generally too polite towards people when they are acting destructively and there are many serious consequences of that. But the anger I am referring to is something else. I see it, as the Tibetans do, as being indicative of a deluded perception.

We use the one word, *anger*, to describe both situations (the destructive form of aggression and the compassionate form of aggression) but this is only because the English language does not equip us to decipher between the two in our speech. This lack of expression in our language then leads to a lack in our emotional awareness because we switch off to the difference in sensation between the two emotions. Most people, in western cultures, are not aware that there even is a difference in internal sensation between compassionately motivated aggression and that anger that is indicative of a distorted perception. It never occurs to them to take notice of it. The Tibetan language, on the other hand, is more well-equipped for describing emotions because the Tibetan culture has grown around Buddhism and its meditation practices. Because of this, there have been enough people in Tibetan culture who were aware of the subtle differences in emotional sensations that they were able to talk about those differences with each other and to see the need to have unique words to decipher between the array of emotions. In Tibetan, the compassionately motivated anger is called *khongtro* while the word *shyédang* refers to hateful anger.

My own definition for anger is:

'Anger (or frustration) is the discomfort that arises when an urgent message from the unconscious mind is being blocked from consciousness. Anger is there to motivate us to search for an alternative idea or perception, not to motivate us to act in anger.'

Pain is not necessarily "bad" in itself. Without pain, you could not keep your body out of danger. When you touch a hot stove, pain lets you know to move your hand away before you are seriously burnt. Negative emotions are painful for the same reason. They motivate us to take action or change our perception.

It seems to me that anger has been misunderstood as if it is meant to prompt the individual to attack. Actually, anger is not intended to motivate us to attack.

Anger is there to draw attention to the deluded, or ineffective perception that we are holding on to. It is uncomfortable for the sake of motivating us to *change* our perception–not for the sake of motivating us to carry on as we are. If it were intended to motivate us to act upon the perception that is already there, then surely it would feel pleasurable. It isn't the anger that is bursting to get out; it's the alternative perception that is bursting to get out.

Have you ever tried to solve a problem and become intensely frustrated only to find after hours of wasted time that you could have fixed the problem much more easily if you had only noticed a different way of doing so? And as soon as that new idea was let through to your conscious mind, the feeling of frustration disappeared, am I right? Because that sensation of frustration was the unconscious mind tapping at your door saying, "I have a message for you". Once you had listened to that sensation and let go of the constraints that your perspective was hammered between, only then was it possible for the message to be brought into awareness. So, contrary to popular belief, forcing through a task in anger does not necessarily aid in overcoming an obstacle.

Really, anger (or frustration) is meant to be useful, but not in the way it is most commonly used. It is meant as a marker rather than a motivator. Anger needs to be uncomfortable if that's what it takes to grab our attention. Anger is brought about by an ineffective view of — or approach to — the situation at hand.

Pigeon-Holing

> *"I do not believe in styles anymore. [...] When you have no style, you say, ok here I am as a human being, now how can I express myself totally and completely? That way you will create a style [your own] as a process of continuing growth."*
>
> —Bruce Lee

In artistry, it can be very limiting and ineffective to bow to the categories that have been set in place through evolving traditions. When the artist places herself in a pigeon-hole, that comes with both advantages and disadvantages. For example, an aspiring songwriter might stick to the category of country music. This makes the whole pursuit of musicianship so much easier to navigate than it would be without a clear genre to conform to as she knows exactly what skills she needs to learn and how and where to get them. She will also know where to market herself and who to network with, and will practically have a template for the whole pursuit. But fitting into a category like this comes with its drawbacks too. In some respect, that country songwriter's creativity will be limited by the constraints of what can be thought of as country music. An alternative approach is to loosen up the category and open up to influence from other genres. By detaching from the label of "country musician", her creative options are freed up. She can then choose the boundaries of her artistry consciously and add elements of other genres as they inspire her.

So, to categorize oneself — which is often an unconscious action — is potentially very limiting. Maybe we do need to think and move within categories at times in order to ease progress, but it's important to be aware of this tendency to categorize and to question whether it really is for the best or whether the categories just appear to be convenient on the surface.

Sophistication

It is said of olives that they are an acquired taste. You won't find many children who love eating olives. They much prefer something sweet. Like grapes. And it's just as well, because olives are bitter and a bitter taste potentially signifies poison in the natural world. For this reason, we are instinctively suspicious of bitter foods when we first encounter them, but with long term exposure to them we can sometimes become unusually partial to them. Even addicted to them. Especially when they are artificially laden with sugar too.

Wine is an example of a bitter food that takes time to develop a taste for. Hence its association with sophistication. When you want to be in a different class to the unsophisticated people—namely, children—it helps to demonstrate that you have a taste for something that no unsophisticated person (child) would take interest in. Hence the practice of wine and cocktail drinking at the high end of town (especially when served with olives).

But sophistication is not only relevant at the high end of town. The other end of town has its own brand of sophistication. Customary displays of sophistication observed at cocktails parties are forms of *overt prestige* while its counterparts observed in dirty pubs are forms of *covert prestige*. Rum is, to the man at the pub, what wine is to the woman at the cocktail party.

In the world of music, sophistication works in much the same way. It is those forms of music that have an acquired taste, such as acid jazz, that we consider to be "sophisticated". It may be no coincidence that its name, *acid* jazz, gives away hints of resemblance to bitterness.

Sophistication is not a full bunk-worthy concept however. There are genuine advantages to sophistication. Many art-forms that are considered to be sophisticated are genuinely valuable. After all, there is a quality to acid jazz that other forms of music can't offer and I'm sure its enthusiasts can verify the value in its qualities and in the culture surrounding it. But sophistication on its own does not *necessarily* signify *better* art. The question really comes back to what is being communicated. For example, if you want to communicate something universal about human relationships to the masses, then a popular style of singer-songwriting may be the best art form. But if you want to experience a more subtle and unusual feeling, maybe more advanced technical skills and a sophisticated art form like jazz will do the job.

The Past

"The image of the thing is not the thing." – Jiddu Krishnamurti

In an artist's lifetime, there are times when she feels she has hit that sweet spot we call being in the zone. It is different to simply going through the motions of playing the song. When the song is played with full sincerity, when the musician *is* the song, the performance is experienced with a quality to it, a realness, that is sensed by the performer as well as by the audience.

Once an artist has felt such an experience there is a tendency to want to repeat it. The musician may think to herself, "I wish I could play it again like I played that day", but, as many artists report, the attempt to repeat the experience *as it was*, always fails. It fails because the want to repeat the experience is not the same as *being* the experience. Or in other words, the memory of the experience is not the *actual* experience. The image of the thing is not the actual thing. The state she was in at that moment when she hit the sweet spot was not a state of wanting to repeat something of the past. She just did it. She *was* the song. Songs say something. She was saying something. That was her approach at the time. Not, "I will perform the song like I did it the other time", but instead, just communicating the song. Being it. Playing it. Enjoying it. Dancing it through.

Instruction

Playing video games can be a surprisingly effective learning experience. When you play a video game with enough skill and focus at some point you may lose yourself in flow. At that moment, you are not thinking in terms of instruction. You are just doing what you are doing. You forget that you are there in front of a screen.

But most of the time when we are going about activities we do not act in this way. We distrust our abilities. We assume that even the simplest tasks require a monotonous level of control. Giving ourselves instructions as if we have split ourselves in two. As if we were there with the game controller, as one self, directing the lesser self. Apparently, there are two of me, and the other half of me doesn't know jack about anything—he needs my instructions for his every move. I push him around all day as if he doesn't know what I know. He is the incompetent one. I know best. All the while, I am neglecting the fact that there is actually only one of me.

There is no part of me that is separate to me. So why can't I just trust it? Why can't I just play everything I do, as if I'm in that video game mode where I'm lost in flow? Why can't I drive my car like that instead of dividing me up as if superior me needs to keep an eye on subordinate me? Can I *be* the whole action rather than looming over myself?

Social Authority

In the pursuit of mastery, we can be led astray by the distortion of our perceptions that social authority creates. There is a common strategy in marketing called *social proofing*. Social proofing occurs when the display of attitudes of higher- or equal-status group members influence an individual's perception. Social proofing can be induced intentionally, for example when a commercial shows attractive people enjoying and worshipping the product being sold. But it can also happen indirectly. An example of this is when a person hears a song on the radio — if they don't know anything about the song they might think it's nothing special. But then they hear that same song in a movie and in a shopping center and at a party, and they hear it was ranked highly on *Rolling Stone*'s Greatest Songs of All Time list. The more they encounter the song in this way, the more social proofing they are receiving regarding the song, and so its prestige is building. After hearing the song in this variety of contexts, the song may begin to appear to be ingenious. For an artist who wants to create work of genuine value, it can be a disaster to fall for social proofing like this. Searching for the qualities in the song that led to its great success might only lead the artist astray because it wasn't necessarily the artwork itself that made the song popular. The song may have risen to that level of popularity by means of social proofing. By worshipping and replicating what is really just a social fad, the artist will waste time creating work that has no value in tomorrow's culture.

A similar situation to the one described above is what I like to call "the vintage effect". That is, the tendency for older works to be valued more highly than recent works. It is often said that music was better in the past than it is today. But those statements are neglecting the vintage effect. When an artwork has aged, it has built up in it a lot of history, social authority and nostalgia. It has stood the test of time, and to some extent, that is impressive in itself. But the idea that older music was better is an illusion, created mostly in this way. (As a side note: the perception that old music was better also comes partly because "old music" encompasses the best songs out of half a century of music while "new music" usually only refers to the past five years at most).

Excessive submission to social authority is one of the biggest killers of innovation. Things that carry social authority can only ever be things that already exist as being popular and accepted. A good way to side-step the hypnotic cage that social authority traps us in is to explore areas that are not considered to be prestigious or valid. The most innovative of the popular musicians are always influenced partly by music genres that are unpopular. By finding the best aspects of those less popular genres and bringing them into play with the qualities of a more popular style of music, they are able to create a fresh sound that a mainstream audience is ready for.

Even in sports, bowing to social authority can stunt performance. The American high jumper Dick Fosbury was laughed at when he began jumping over the bar in such an awkward way. Nowadays, the "Fosbury flop" is the standard method in high jump.

The key to avoiding the rut of submission to social authority is to bring the focus back to creating true value. Rather than trying to *be something*, why not aim to *do something*. If you're making music, your aim is most likely to communicate something to the listener. If you're playing tennis, you want to win beautifully. If you're designing a house, your aim might be to design a house that creates a good vibe. By focusing on the task at hand without needing to impress or to blindly fit in, the constraints of social authority are lifted and innovation is made possible.

Submission to social authority doesn't just hinder innovation; it also stands in the way of enjoyment. The flow state is a rare occurrence for people who believe they need social authority to instruct their every move.[35] Some people only seem to appreciate sights and experiences that are accepted as being valid and glamorous, like seeing the Eiffel Tower, for example. But these experiences are not necessarily any better than the happenings that we are fortunate enough to witness on an ordinary day. Many things can be seen as being more miraculous and entertaining than famous monuments and landmarks if we take off the distorting lens of social

authority.

Aversion to Solitude

"The fear of rejection when one wants acceptance can cripple initiative and negate personal autonomy."[36]
—Psychologist, Philip Zimbardo, creator of the famous Stanford Prison Experiment

"All of humanity's problems stem from man's inability to sit quietly in a room alone."
—Blaise Pascal

"In technological societies, we spend about one third of the day alone, a much greater proportion than in most tribal societies, where being alone is often considered to be very dangerous."[37]
—Mihaly Csikszentmihalyi

A person who strongly dislikes being alone will have difficulty in developing one of the most important character attributes of an innovator — the potential to employ initiative. The pursuit of mastery will inevitably involve periods spent in solitude while thinking, reading, and practicing, as skills and understanding are developed and deepened. Fear of solitude is one of the strongest fears across all people, though it does not affect everyone. And for most people, it can be quickly reduced through a better understanding of the nature of loneliness.

Loneliness seems like a simple matter on the surface. The assumption is that if a person is not paired up, or if they have few friends around to keep them company, then they must be lonely. But when loneliness is looked at more closely it isn't as straightforward as that.

Many people who are married with children are still very lonely, while on the other hand, there are many people who live in solitude and are not lonely. Romance doesn't always cure loneliness; it can often exacerbate it (suddenly the person feels insecure when their partner is gone for just a day). And most people tend to feel much lonelier when they are in the wrong company than when they are alone in their own company. Stranger still, if solitude is chosen intentionally, it doesn't carry any sensation of loneliness with it.

So, what is loneliness then, if it's not always cured by close relationships? For sure, it's understandable that people hold this fear. But in many people, it's a little over-the-top. As far as the pursuit of mastery is concerned, usually a person would only need to be able to relax in their own company for a matter of hours without freaking out. It's surprising how rare that ability is, considering that nobody who cares about you now is going to forget about you any time soon. But fortunately, the ability to relax in solitude is one that can be developed through intentional exposure.

The Final Foundation of Flow

Non-Duality

"I can't really explain what it's like except in a physical sense. It's a massive rush of adrenaline, which comes at a certain point. Usually it's a sharing experience; it's not something I could experience on my own [...] It's not even just the musicians: it's everyone that's involved in the whole experience. Everyone in that place seems to unify at one point. It's when you get that completely harmonic experience, where everyone is hearing exactly the same thing without any interpretation whatsoever or any kind of angle. They're all transported toward the same place [...] You could call it unity, which is a very spiritual word for me. Everyone is one at that point, at that specific point in time, not for very long. Of course, the minute you become aware of that it's gone."

—Eric Clapton

There is one last foundational aspect of the flow state that brings all this together, capturing the essence of peak performance and enjoyment. That is—*non-dual perception*. When the mind's focus is split, energy is dissipated and mental processing is stunted due to the interference that is caused by distractions. It is only when the mind is operating in a *non-dual* state that flow occurs. In such a state, performance peaks, as does enjoyment.

Non-dual action was perfectly described in Timothy Gallwey's landmark work of sports psychology, *The Inner Game of Tennis*. Here, he uses the analogy of a cat hunting its prey:

> Effortlessly alert, he crouches, gathering his relaxed muscles for the spring. Not thinking about when to jump, nor how he will push off with his hind legs to attain the proper distance, his mind is

still and perfectly concentrated on his prey. No thought flashes into his consciousness of the possibility or consequences of missing his mark. He sees only bird. Suddenly the bird takes off; at the same instant, the cat leaps. With perfect anticipation, he intercepts his dinner two feet off the ground. Perfectly, thoughtlessly executed action, and afterward, no self-congratulations, just the reward inherent in his action: the bird in his mouth.[38]

As this classic statement describes, non-dual action is effortless action. Although the movement may be swift and precise, on a psychological level, there is no effort being exerted. There is no sense of struggle. No display put on with the intention to impress. No thought of technique. No ideology. The person does not sense that the act is heroic in any way. As there is no sense of 'Self', flow is an observer-less state. The movement occurs via an automatic process, without a motive-to-an-end in mind.

In many situations, an excessive attempt at conscious control of the activity would only interfere with performance. Rather than consciously thinking about technique, it would be far more effective to allow the activity to be executed by the instinctual reflexes, some of which are inherent in our nature and others that have been built through the process of mastery. D.T. Suzuki said it with grace in his foreword to *Zen in the Art of Archery*.

As soon as we reflect, deliberate, and conceptualize, the original unconsciousness is lost and a thought interferes... the arrow is off the string but does not fly straight to the target, nor does the target stand where it is. Calculation, which is miscalculation sets in [...]

Man is a thinking reed but his best works are done when he is not calculating and thinking. "Childlikeness" has to be restored.[39]

Aside from enhanced performance, a further benefit of the non-dual state is that anxiety is reduced. Much of the time, anxiety results from running on split-focus. Trying to execute a difficult activity while the mind is distracted by other thoughts, this seems to create a lot of nervous turbulence and anxiety. It may be that in these situations, anxiety is the body's way of getting our attention by making us uncomfortable with the way we're doing things, so that we will learn a more effective way of living. As if it were saying, "Hey, you're running two situations at once here — the one in your head and the one in front of you. This isn't easy for me".

The artist can reduce such interference by remaining present. This is another reason why, as mentioned earlier, an artist does not necessarily benefit from being *obsessed* with their craft. When the craft moves from being an interest to being an obsession, that creates a duality in all other activities in the artist's life as he will be constantly running on split-focus while doing anything other than the craft itself. There may be benefits to such an obsession, but there comes a time to question whether the obsession is merely a form of escapism that is creating more problems than it's solving. This is certainly not to say that it's "wrong" for an artist to work diligently for long hours on his craft. But there is a difference between doing so with good reason and doing so out of an uncontrollable — and perhaps unwanted —

obsession. Concentration, on its own, is not necessarily virtuous. Jon Kabat-Zinn puts it well in his book, *Wherever You Go, There You Are*:

> Concentration can be of great value, but it can also be seriously limiting if you become seduced by the pleasant quality of this inner experience and come to see it as a refuge from life in an unpleasant and unsatisfactory world. You might be tempted to avoid the messiness of daily living for the tranquility of stillness and peacefulness. This, of course, would be an attachment to stillness, and like any strong attachment, it leads to delusion. It arrests development and short-circuits the cultivation of wisdom.[40]

After reading this book, on the surface, the process toward mastery may seem contrived. But the beauty becomes apparent when you realize that it's only in those moments when the artist has given up on the pursuit that sincere works then appear. Sincere action, in any endeavor, can only really happen spontaneously. If sincerity is made an aim, then that implies that the person doing the aiming is *not* sincere to begin with. And so, it is contradictory to make sincerity a goal. This concept was well known in ancient times. The Second-Century Buddhist philosopher Nagarjuna criticized the search for purity. Philosopher, David Loy, explains this paradox:

> The implication of Nagarjuna's argument is that attempting to live a pure life involves a preoccupation with impurity. In order to have only pure thoughts and actions, one must avoid

impure ones, and this means determining to which of the two categories each thought and action belongs. It is generally claimed that this dichotomizing tendency of mind keeps us from experiencing situations as they really are in themselves, when no such dualistic categories as pure and impure, good and bad and so on are applicable.[41]

When sincerity is seen in a work of art, there is a sense of having sincerity contained and with that comes a sense of security. But I do wonder if that attempt to bottle sincerity is really just something we do out of fear. Maybe we are afraid to look for sincerity in the actions of everyday life because, as Nagarjuna pointed out, when we search for purity, we have to distinguish between what is pure and what is not. We are then engulfed in a painful thought process, day in day out, frequently seeing "wrongness" and invalidity in the world around us.

"When people drop the good-bad, strong-weak thinking that grows out of the fixed mindset, they're better able to learn useful strategies that help with self-control [...] It's like anything else in the growth mindset. It's a reminder that you're an unfinished human being and a clue to how to do it better next time."—Carol Dweck, psychologist

"...one of the strongest motives that lead men to art and science is escape from everyday life with its painful crudity and hopeless dreariness, from the fetters of one's own ever-shifting desires. A finely tempered nature longs to escape from the personal life into the world of objective perception and thought."

—Albert Einstein

So, the search for sincerity isn't what it seems. And, in a similar notion, we cannot force effortless action, because that would be trying not to try, which, of course, is still trying. So, what can we do to make *flow* a more common occurrence in our lives and in our arts despite these dilemmas? The answer, I believe, is to follow curiosity and to realize the value of fun. If an activity is genuinely fun, then it will provide an easier way to slip into the flow state because the foundations of flow will be there automatically — the activity will be an end in itself, and therefore it will be effortless.

Different things seem like fun to different people and at different times depending on their skills and interests. I believe that this is a reflection of the fundamental nature of the mind. It seems to me, that the unconscious sorts out what would be the best opportunity to explore next, but it can't deliver the answer in clear and logical language because the explanation may be too complex to put into words. So instead, the unconscious mind delivers its brain mail in the form of an intuitive sensation. And, when it comes to creative pursuits and artistry, that brain mail is a sense of curiosity and adventure. To follow that curiosity demands the endurance of situations that are guaranteed to make a person look clumsy and feel a little out of place at first, as they journey into the unknown. Who knows where that might lead. The process may be a reward in itself.

"To me, ultimately martial art means honestly expressing yourself. It is very difficult to do. I mean it is easy for me to put on a show and be cocky and be flattered with a cocky feeling [...] Or I can make all kinds of phony things — you know what I mean — and blind you by it. Or I can show you some really fancy movement.

But to express oneself honestly — not lying to oneself —

to express myself honestly, my friend, is very hard to do.

And you have to train. you have to keep your reflexes so

that when you want it, it's there."

—Bruce Lee

Contact

To contact or to join the email list please write to:

counterintuitivethought@gmail.com

By joining the email list, you will be notified of future book releases and music record releases.

Follow the writing and music of Jax Pax at:

@jaxpaxworx on Instagram

Recommended Resources

Flow: The Psychology of Optimal Experience

Written by Mihaly Csikszentmihalyi, the psychologist who first recognized and named the flow state, this book has influenced many artists, athletes, thinkers and business people around the world. The term *flow* has since become common in everyday language as a result of this author's work.

TheFlowChannel.com

Theflowchannel.com is a website dedicated to educating people about flow and how it can be applied in everyday life. The website features a podcast hosted by expert flow researchers.

Tribe of Mentors: Short Life Advice from the Best in the World

Tim Ferriss's book Tribe of Mentors is full of quick-to-access advice from more than 100 successful people. There is a gem on every page and, like all of Tim's books, it will lead you toward many other books and learning experiences that are of high quality. This is another book that can be read in spare moments rather than requiring a large time investment.

The Inner Game of Tennis: The Classic Guide to the Mental Side of Peak Performance

The Inner Game of Tennis is the first book from a full series of 'Inner Game' books including: *The Inner Game of Skiing, The Inner Game of Work, The Inner Game of Stress, The Inner Game of Music and The Inner Game of Golf.* These titles are basically Zen philosophy in a nutshell yet with barely a mention of Zen. For anyone who is interested in learning more about Zen principles without having to spend time studying folklore or meditation, this series is very useful. *The Inner Game of Tennis* was published in the 70's and is still one of the highest selling books on sports psychology.

Mindset (updated edition): Changing the Way You Think to Fulfil Your Potential

I only touched on Carol Dweck's work briefly in this book. If you want to know more about the growth mindset and how it can be used to advantage in education and in relationships this is the most important book on the subject.

The Art of Learning

Josh Waitzkin was mentioned several times throughout this book as *The Art of Learning* had quite an impact on me. It was also the inspiration behind Tim Ferriss's book

The Four-Hour Chef. Josh Waitzkin was a world champion at chess and then went onto become world champion at the martial art, Tai Chi Push Hands, despite having been up against people who had been trained from an early age to become champions at the sport. He did so by using learning principles he had learnt from chess, such as condensed practice, focusing on the fundamentals and focusing on finishing positions amongst others. Half biography, half instructional, *The Art of Learning* is very inspiring and beautifully written.

Peak: How All of Us Can Achieve Extraordinary Things

This is a fascinating read that goes into the science of peak performance and details the educations of various high performers. The book discusses what gives world class performers their competitive edge.

Proko – YouTube Channel

The *Proko* YouTube channel is a series of podcasts and instructional videos hosted by the brilliant professional art teachers, Stan Prokopenko and Marshall Vandruff. It is an excellent resource for anyone wanting to develop as an artist, especially professionally, and especially as a visual artist or draftsman, but musicians could benefit greatly from the podcast too.

Acknowledgements

Grateful Acknowledgement is made to the following authors for use of extracts and information from their books and articles, which I recommend reading to deepen your understanding of the content covered in this book.

---

[1] **Reprinted from *Flow: The Psychology of Optimal Experience* (1990) by Mihaly Csikszentmihalyi with permission of HarperCollins Publishers, www.harpercollins.com/**

[2] **Reprinted from *Tools of Titans: The Tactics, Routines, and Habits of Billionaires, Icons, and World-Class Performers* (2016) by Timothy Ferriss, with permission of Penguin Random House UK, London, United Kingdom, www.penguin.co.uk/**

[3] **Mihaly Csickszentmihalyi, *Flow: The Psychology of Optimal Experience* (HarperCollins Publishers, 1990), www.harpercollins.com/**

[4] **Reprinted from *Finding Flow: The Psychology of Optimal Experience* (1990) by Mihaly Csikszentmihalyi with permission of HarperCollins Publishers, www.harpercollins.com/**

[5] **Reprinted from *The Art of Learning* (2008) by Josh Waitzkin, with permission of Simon and Schuster,**

New York, www.simonandschuster.com/

[6] Reprinted from *Peak: Secrets from the New Science of Expertise* (2016) by K. Anders Ericsson and Robert Pool, Bodley Head, with permission of The Random House Group Ltd

[7] Judit Polgar, Biography (Accessed 2017) by Judit Polgar, www.juditpolgar.com/

[8] Linnet Myers, *Trained to Be a Genius, Girl, 16, Wallops Champ Spassky for $110,000* (Chicago Tribune, Februrary 18, 1993) http://articles.chicagotribune.com/1993-02-18/news/9303181339_1_judit-polgar-boris-spassky-world-chess-champion, accessed June 15, 2017)

[9] Andrew J. Waters, Fernand Gobet, and Gerv Layden, *Visuospatial Abilities in Chess Players* (British Journal of Psychology 93, 2002): 557-565

[10] Roland H. Grabner, Aljoscha C. Neubauer, and Elbeth Stern, *Superior Performance and Neural Efficiency: The Impact of Intelligence and Expertise* (Brain Research Bulletin 69, 2006): 422-439

[11] Francesca Happe, and Pedro Vital, *What Aspects of Autism Predispose to Talent?* (Philosophical Transaction of The Royal Society B 364, no. 1522, 2009): 1369-1375

[12] Walter Isaacson, *Einstein: His Life and Universe* (London: Simon and Schuster, 2007)

[13] Walter Isaacson, *Einstein: His Life and Universe* (London: Simon and Schuster, 2007)

[14] Walter Isaacson, *Einstein: His Life and Universe* (London: Simon and Schuster, 2007)

[15] V.S. Ramachandran, *The Tell-Tale Brain: Unlocking the Mystery of Human Nature* (London: Windmill Books, 2011)

[16] Carol S. Dweck, *Mindset (updated edition): Changing the Way You Think to Fulfil Your Potential* (London: Little Brown Book Group, 2006)

[17] Reprinted from *Mindset (updated edition): Changing the Way You Think to Fulfil Your Potential* (2006) by Carol S. Dweck, Little Brown Book Group, www.littlebrown.co.uk/

[18] Reprinted from *Tools of Titans: The Tactics, Routines, and Habits of Billionaires, Icons, and World-Class Performers* (2016) by Timothy Ferriss, with permission of Penguin Random House UK, London, United Kingdom, www.penguin.co.uk/

[19] Reprinted from *The Mindful Athlete: Secrets to Pure Performance* (2015) by George Mumford with permission of Parallax Press, Berkeley, California,

www.parallax.org/

[20] Reprinted from *Tools of Titans: The Tactics, Routines, and Habits of Billionaires, Icons, and World-Class Performers* (2016) by Timothy Ferriss, with permission of Penguin Random House UK, London, United Kingdom, www.penguin.co.uk/

[21] Reprinted from *The Art of Learning* (2008) by Josh Waitzkin, with permission of Simon and Schuster, New York, www.simonandschuster.com/

[22] Bruce Lee, Tao of Jeet Kune Do (Chicago: Black Belt Communications, 2011)

[23] Timothy Ferriss, *The Four-Hour Chef: The Simple Path to Cooking Like a Pro, Learning Anything and Living the Good Life* (Las Vegas: Amazon Publishing, 2012)

[24] Pat Pattison, *Co-Writing: The "No" Free Zone* (Pattison, 2009) www.patpattison.com/cowriting/

[25] Reprinted from *The Mindful Athlete: Secrets to Pure Performance* (2015) by George Mumford with permission of Parallax Press, Berkeley, California, www.parallax.org/

[26] Mark Synnott with Alex Honnold, *Exclusive: Climber Completes the Most Dangerous Rope-Free Ascent Ever* (National Geographic Partners, LLC, June 3, 2017)

[27] Reprinted from *Full Catastrophe Living: Using the Wisdom of Your Body and Mind to Face Stress, Pain, and Illness* (2013) by Jon Kabat-Zinn with permission of Little Brown Book Group, www.littlebrown.co.uk/

[28] Shunryu Suzuki, *Zen Mind Beginners Mind: Informal Talks on Zen Meditation and Practice* (Weatherhill, 1970)

[29] Reprinted from *Full Catastrophe Living: Using the Wisdom of Your Body and Mind to Face Stress, Pain, and Illness* (2013) by Jon Kabat-Zinn with permission of Little Brown Book Group, www.littlebrown.co.uk/

[30] Reprinted from *The Miracle of Mindfulness: A Manual on Meditation* (Boston: Beacon Press, 1996) by Thich Nhat Hanh

[31] Edward de Bono, www.edwarddebonofoundation.com (copyright, 2014)

[32] David Loy, *Nonduality: A Study in Comparative Philosophy* (Humanity Books, 1988)

[33] V.S. Ramachandran, and Robert Greene, *Interviews with the Masters: A Companion to Robert Greene's Mastery* (Robert Greene, 2013)

[34] Reprinted from *Born for Love: Why Empathy is Essential and Endangered* (William Morrow

Paperbacks, 2011) by Bruce Perry

[35] Mihaly Csickszentmihalyi, *Flow: The Psychology of Optimal Experience* (HarperCollins Publishers, 1990), www.harpercollins.com/

[36] Reprinted from *The Lucifer Effect: Understanding How Good People Turn Evil* (Penguin Random House, 2008) by Philip Zimbardo

[37] Reprinted from *Flow: The Psychology of Optimal Experience* (1990) by Mihaly Csikszentmihalyi with permission of HarperCollins Publishers, www.harpercollins.com

[38] Reprinted from *The Inner Game of Tennis: The Classic Guide to the Mental Side of Peak Performance* (1974) by Timothy Gallwey, Penguin Random House UK, London, United Kingdom, www.penguin.co.uk/

[39] D.T. Suzuki, and Eugen Herrigel, *Zen in the Art of Archery* (Routledge, 1953)

[40] Reprinted from *Wherever You Go There You Are: Mindfulness Meditation in Everyday Life* (1994) by Jon Kabat-Zinn with permission of Little Brown Book Group, www.littlebrown.co.uk/

[41] Reprinted from *Nonduality: A Study in Comparative Philosophy* (1988) by David Loy, Humanity books